The Curious Girl's Book of Adventure

The Curious Girl's Book of Adventure

Claire Gillman

This Modern Books edition published by Elwin Street Productions.

Conceived and produced by
Elwin Street Limited
144 Liverpool Road
London N1 1LA
www.elwinstreet.com

Cover design by Tony Palmer © Penguin Group (Australia)
Internal design: Thomas Keenes
Internal illustrations: David Eaton
Cover illustration: Brian Clinton

ISBN: 978-0-9556421-4-2

Printed in Singapore

To my special girls: Alice, Amy and Kate Alger-Green; Rosalind and Eleanor Gillman; and Becky and Amy Marr – may you always remain curious and your lives full of adventure!

As ever, I'd like to thank my husband Nick and my two sons Alex and George for their unswerving support, particularly as deadlines loomed, and my editor Dan Mills for making the writing of this book so much fun.

Contents

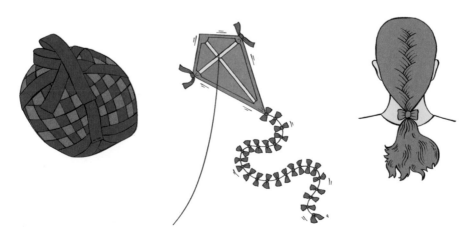

Introduction

TOO OFTEN IN THE PAST, when it came to adventuring, boys got to do all the fun stuff and girls didn't get a look in. We were left behind and told to take up more gentle pursuits, such as needlework or playing the piano.

Thank goodness those days are long gone! Now, a curious girl can take on as much adventure as she can handle – it's just a question of knowing where to look and getting some insight into how to do these exciting activities safely and successfully.

That's where this book comes in. It's designed and written for girls with a keen sense of adventure, whatever your age and wherever you live. Whether you're a fresh air junkie looking for outdoor challenges, such as making yourself a shelter, tracking animals or lighting a fire, or you're more of an indoor adventurer, who loves telling ghost stories, juggling or performing card tricks, there's bound to be something in these pages that's just right for you.

And you'll be surprised when you read how simple and fun adventuring can be. You may well find yourself wanting to try out some activities that it had never before crossed your mind to attempt. Former shrinking violets may find themselves eager to get on the karaoke machine after reading the Performing chapter, and those who've always had an aversion to cooking may be amazed to find that they make the best smoothies in town after reading chapter four! Approach every topic with an open mind,

like all great adventurers, and who knows where you might
end up?

Although we give a passing nod to the techno whizzes among
you by suggesting ways to create a web page, in the main, this
book attempts to get away from the computer screens and video
gaming that occupy so many girls' after-school hours, and back
into the habit of making your own fun. With a few simple
props and ingredients, you can create hours of adventure and
entertainment, and what's more, many of these adventures are
fun to share with your best friends.

So, if you have a curious mind, and you're ready for adventure
and excitement, the fun starts right here. Read on!

How to use this book

Some of the adventures included in the following chapters are
more difficult than others, so you may need a helping hand.
Every activity is graded for difficulty, as you will see, by the
number of symbols underneath the title. One-symbol projects
are for solo adventurers. Two-symbol projects might take a little
more time and could need someone else to help out. Three-
symbol projects are serious adventures.

⚠ Any projects marked with this symbol involve the use of tools,
fire or other elements that may be dangerous. Always make sure
an adult knows what you're doing and is around to help out with
these projects.

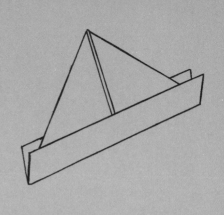

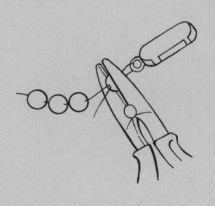

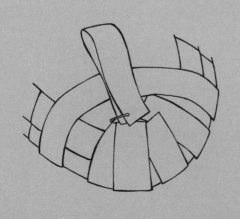

Chapter One

Creating

IF YOU'VE GOT AN ENQUIRING MIND and you like to get absorbed in what you're doing, then this is the chapter for you. It's packed full of ideas for things to make, some just for fun, and some that'll be useful and could even last you a lifetime. There's something to fit every taste and every timescale.

◆

You can while away a rainy afternoon pressing flowers, drawing a comic strip or making greetings cards; or spend a few days on the grander projects, like making clay pots, writing a play, creating your own jewellery or even decorating your bedroom.

◆

And you're not limited to being creative indoors either: there are tips on growing sunflowers and herbs, and taking cool photographs of you and your friends. There's so much to choose from, so let's get started!

Friendship bracelets

✦✦✦

To give your best friends a bracelet that you have designed and made specially for them is a token of friendship that speaks louder than words. Here's a great pattern for the perfect friendship bracelet for your best mates.

YOU WILL NEED
- 4 50-cm (20-in) lengths of embroidery thread in two different colours
- Pins and a board (optional)
- Lots of time!

STEPS

1 TAKE YOUR THREADS (two purple and two green, for example) and lay them out in alternatating colours.

2 FOLD ALL THE THREADS IN HALF. Then, holding just below where the threads bend over, tie a knot in the bunch of threads so they're all held together by a loop at the top. Some beginners put a pin through this loop to hold it to a board while they work – it's up to you whether or not you try this.

3 YOU ARE NOW READY TO START WEAVING. Fan out the loose threads so that you have eight ends in alternating colours.

4 START WITH THE OUTER THREADS. Take the left-hand thread (which is purple) and make a knot around the green thread next to it by passing it in front of the green thread and then around the back, bringing it out so that it crosses in front of itself.

④

5 THEN, TAKE IT OVER THE FRONT of the green thread again, around the back, bring it up through the loop that you've created and pull the knot tight.

6 REPEAT THIS ON BOTH SIDES so that, effectively, your two outer threads have each moved one place towards the middle.

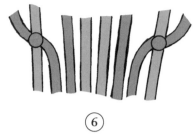

6

7 CONTINUE TO MAKE KNOTS towards the middle using the same two threads. When they meet, knot them together.

8 NOW REPEAT STEPS 3–6 with the new outer threads. You should start to build up chevrons (V-shapes) in alternating colours as you tie more and more knots.

9 KEEP REPEATING THE KNOTS until the bracelet is long enough to fit around your wrist.

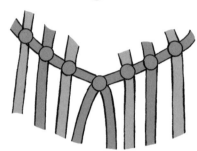

7

10 ONCE THE BRACELET IS LONG ENOUGH, gather all the ends of the threads together and tie them in a knot as you did at the start.

11 FIND A FRIEND YOU LIKE ENOUGH to give the bracelet to, and get them to hold out their wrist. Loop the bracelet around it, and pass the loose ends from where you finished the bracelet through the little loop you made when you started.

12 TIE THE LOOSE ENDS ROUND THE LOOP to secure the bracelet. *Et voilà* – a beautiful friendship bracelet that your closest friends are bound to love!

A kaleidoscope

✦✦✦

Of all the things you can create, the kaleidoscope may not be the most practical, but it is one of the prettiest. And it makes a lovely present for a baby sister – if you can bear to part with it!

YOU WILL NEED

- Cardboard
- Tracing paper
- Scissors
- 3 small rectangular mirrors
- Clear adhesive tape

- A pencil
- Small, shiny pieces of paper or cellophane cut into shapes
- About an hour's worth of free time

STEPS

1 PLACE A MIRROR ON A SHEET OF CARDBOARD and, keeping as close to the edge of the mirror as possible, trace around it using a pencil. Repeat with the other two mirrors.

2 CUT OUT THE CARDBOARD along the pencil lines so that you have three rectangular pieces of cardboard the same size as your mirrors.

3 USING THE ADHESIVE TAPE, stick the mirrors to the cardboard pieces (try to get only the barest amount of tape on the front of the mirrors or it will show up in your kaleidoscope).

4 WITH THE MIRRORS ON THE INSIDE, tape the three pieces tightly together to form a triangular tube.

5 CUT OUT TWO TRIANGULAR PIECES of tracing paper to fit over the end of the triangular tube. Then tape two of the three sides of the tracing paper triangles together to make a triangular pocket.

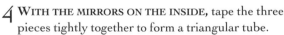

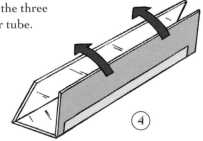

④

6 FILL THIS POCKET with small bits of shiny paper pieces (don't put in too many or they won't be able to move freely).

7 NOW TAPE SHUT THE THIRD SIDE so the shiny bits of paper are sealed inside. Then tape the triangle over one end of the triangular tube.

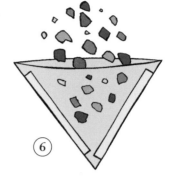

8 CUT OUT A TRIANGULAR PIECE of cardboard to fit over the opposite end of the tube, and tape it in place.

9 USING YOUR PENCIL, carefully poke an eyehole into the triangular cardboard end-piece.

10 RAISE THE TUBE TOWARDS THE LIGHT and look through the eyehole. The light reflects off the mirrors and creates gorgeous symmetrical patterns – and every time you shake your kaleidoscope and look again, there's a wonderful new pattern.

11 YOU CAN DECORATE THE OUTSIDE of your kaleidoscope with paints, crayons, sequins or anything you like to make it look attractive. This is particularly nice if you're giving it as a gift.

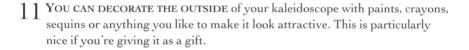

DID YOU KNOW? A Scottish scientist called David Brewster is often credited with inventing the kaleidoscope in 1816. In fact, it was originally an invention of the ancient Greek mathematicians, but their secret was lost in the mists of time.

Your own web page

✦✦✦

You might think that the Internet is the preserve of techno whizz-kids, nerds and geeks, but think again. Now you can make a bold statement about yourself by creating your very own web page.

If you're a techno-babe, then you'll already know all about writing and designing in computer languages and so on. But for most of us, it all sounds like gibberish. That doesn't mean that the less IT-minded of us can't have fun on the Web too, though. There are many sites today that allow you to log into a members' area and use on-line editors to create your very own web page. Some of the major search engines offer this same service – check them out. Once you've found a site that you like, there are just a few things to bear in mind before designing your page . . .

YOU WILL NEED

- A computer
- Your imagination

STEPS

1 CHOOSE WHICH SITE YOU WANT TO USE. Have a look through the options and see what they offer. Do you just want a straightforward blog (a sort of on-line diary)? Or do you want something more grand and complicated, with pictures or even music?

2 GIVE PLENTY OF THOUGHT to what you want to say on your site. Of course, it could be all about you – or it could be on a subject close to your heart, such as a favourite hobby, an issue that you want to promote like protecting the environment, or a band or sports team.

3 FIRST IMPRESSIONS COUNT, so make sure it's easy for a visitor to identify what your page is all about. A good way to do this is to give it a title and sub-titles to break up the text into bitesize chunks, which are easy for your readers to digest.

4 GRAPHICS (IMAGES) CAN ADD GREAT PIZZAZZ to a page and stop people getting bored trawling through endless lines of text. You may want to create your own graphics using a drawing and/or animation programme.

5 SOME SITES LET YOU UPLOAD photos, music or even videos. If you're in a band this can be a great way to reach an audience! Just remember that anyone can access the information you're uploading, so don't give away anything too personal.

WARNING

If you use pictures of yourself or your friends, remember that all sorts of people will be visiting your page, so use your discretion. Never give away details of your home address and never arrange to meet Internet friends in real life unless someone responsible comes with you.

6 ONCE YOU'VE DECIDED what you want to include, plan it out on a sheet of paper so you know exactly where it's all going to go. Then start building your site on the Internet.

7 YOU CAN PLAY WITH THE TEXT, using different font sizes, colours and typefaces, rather than having everything in the same old styles. But don't get too carried away – ultimately, your audience must be able to read what you've written.

8 NEVER TAKE IMAGES OR TEXT from another site unless you're sure it's ok to use. Most of the stuff on the web is copyright, and you must get permission to use it or you could end up being sued.

9 ONCE YOU'RE SATISFIED with your design, upload it to your chosen host site and you're away! Just remember to tell all your friends about it so they can come and visit.

An origami boat

⚜ ⚜

The hobby of folding paper, more commonly known as origami, goes back many centuries. Although paper was introduced to Japan from China in the sixth century, folding paper to make models only became popular in the 1600s. The earliest designs were simple and started with boats and boxes, but now origami enthusiasts can make the most intricate and beautiful models of flowers, animals and birds – and all without the use of a single pin, spot of glue or staple!

You too can make some amazing models ranging from trinket boxes to diamonds (well they are a girl's best friend) and paper roses, using only paper, your hands and some nifty folding. As a newcomer to origami, you may find it a little fiddly at first but, with a little practice, you'll be making beautiful models in no time. Let's start for now with something simple. How about a paper boat fit to sail any pond, stream or puddle?

YOU WILL NEED

- A large sheet of rectangular coloured paper – the brighter the better!

STEPS

1 FOLD THE PAPER IN HALF WIDTHWAYS and make a crisp crease in the middle.

2 BRING EACH OF THE TOP CORNERS in to meet in the middle, forming a triangular point. Crease the folds so that it lays flat.

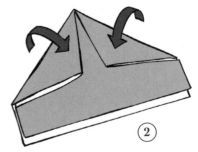

3 FOLD THE BOTTOM EDGE UPWARDS, so that the fold is level with the bottom of the triangle. Then flip it over and fold the other edge up in the same way.

4 HOLD THE TRIANGLE POINT-DOWN, with your thumbs inside, and pull it open so that the sides come together. Press them flat and you should be left with a diamond shape.

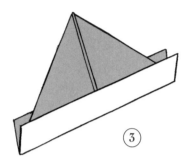

(3)

5 AT THE OPEN END of the diamond, fold each side down to make another triangle. Then pull it open as you did before to make another diamond.

6 NEARLY THERE! Now all you have to do is turn the diamond upside-down and pull the sides away from the middle. With a little careful shaping, you'll end up with a beautiful paper boat with high prow and stern, and a triangular mast.

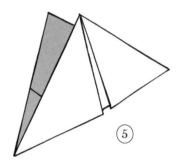

(5)

DID YOU KNOW? Paper folding was not always called 'origami' in Japan. Until the 1800s it was known as 'orikata' or 'orimono'. In the late 1800s the hobby fell out of vogue and it wasn't revived until the 1950s when a Japanese man called Akira Yoshikawa started to publish books with new models and designs.

To ensure you get a neat-looking model, make the folds as crisp as possible by running your fingernail along the edge to flatten the fold, and keep the corners neat by using the tip of your nail or a ballpoint pen to guide the fold to produce a sharp edge.

A clay pot

These attractive pots can be used for storing jewellery on your dressing table, keeping little treasures safe or even for holding sweets on a coffee table. And you'll never see another one the same as yours!

YOU WILL NEED
- Air-dried or home-oven fired clay
- An apron or old shirt (to protect your clothes)
- Poster paints
- Decorations, e.g. fake gems, baubles, glitter, etc. (optional)

STEPS

1 GET HOLD OF SOME POTTER'S CLAY. The type used by professional potters needs to be fired (baked) at very high temperatures, but you can buy hobby clay from craft stores that will either dry by itself or can be baked in a home oven. This project can get messy, so put on an apron or overall to cover your clothes, and make sure you have a hard, flat surface to work on – one that won't stain.

2 WARM THE CLAY BY KNEADING IT with your hands. If you keep folding it over on top of itself, you will create air bubbles (which you want to avoid) so after kneading, throw the ball backwards and forwards quite roughly between your hands or throw it onto a hard surface (like a worktop) several times.

3 ONCE THE CLAY IS SOFT AND PLIABLE, roll it into a long 'worm' that's about 12 mm (½ an inch) in diameter and about 30–60 cm (12–24 inches) long. Keep the width of the worm as consistent as possible all the way down – you don't want any bulges in your pot.

4 TAKE ONE END OF THE 'WORM' and start to coil it into a tight circle. Continue to coil it around itself until you've created a circular base for your pot, making sure the coils are pressed together. (You can even mould them into a smooth base by scraping a straight edge across the surface.) Cut the 'worm' where the coil finishes, and secure the end by moulding it onto the coil.

5 NOW YOU CAN START THE SIDES OF THE POT. Take the end of your clay 'worm' and coil it around the outside of the base. Press it down firmly and then, on the inside of your pot (while supporting the outside wall with the other hand so it doesn't bow out), smooth down with your fingertips to seal the gap between the bottom and the coil.

6 AS YOU REACH THE END OF THE FIRST COIL, allow the worm to overlap and continue building the wall, smoothing down each time.

7 ONCE YOU'VE REACHED THE DESIRED HEIGHT (or the end of your worm), level out the top row by flattening it down slightly and trimming down the end.

8 MAKE SURE THE INSIDE is completely smoothed out – wetting your fingers makes this easier.

9 IF YOU ARE HAVING TROUBLE REMOVING YOUR POT from the work surface, take a piece of string and wrap it around a couple of fingers on both hands (rather like dental floss) and, pulling the string tight, 'saw' the string back and forth, pulling it towards you underneath the pot.

10 IF YOU'RE USING HOME-OVEN CLAY, then follow the instructions that came with it to bake it solid. This clay is best baked on an oven-safe glass surface. For air-dry clay, just leave the pot out overnight until it hardens.

11 ONCE YOUR CLAY IS FULLY DRY, you can paint the pot. Put on two coats, and glue on any other decorations you fancy.

A basket

❖❖❖

The basket weaving art form is one of the oldest known crafts, even pre-dating pottery making, and the skill has been handed down through the generations. Although it's probably a bit too ambitious to attempt to make a traditional willow basket from scratch, you can start with a paper basket to get the hang of the principles and then work your way up to the real thing (kits are available from craft shops if you want to cheat a little).

YOU WILL NEED
- 2 large sheets of construction paper in different colours (say green and red)
- Stapler or craft glue
- Nimble fingers

STEPS

1 CUT EACH SHEET OF PAPER INTO LONG STRIPS about 12 mm (½ an inch) wide. Lay out 12 strips of the same colour (red, for example) next to each other in vertical lines, then count out 12 strips of the other colour (we'll say green for this example).

2 TAKE A GREEN STRIP and, starting about a third of the way down, horizontally weave it over the first vertical red strip on the right and under the next, repeating this over and under movement until you reach the other side. Pull the strip through so that you have roughly equal ends protruding on each side of the vertical strips.

3 TAKE THE NEXT GREEN STRIP and weave it horizontally through the red vertical strips starting just below your first green strip.

4 CONTINUE WEAVING THE STRIPS until all 12 green strips have been used.

5 TRY TO KEEP THE WEAVING NEAT AND EVEN so that you end up with a reasonably tight chequerboard effect.

6 YOU SHOULD NOW HAVE A WOVEN BASE with green strips extending on two opposite sides and red strips extending on the other two opposite sides.

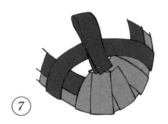

7 GATHER UP THE STRIPS ON ONE SIDE. Bend them upwards and collect into the middle to form a fan shape that is broader at the base so that all the ends come together. Staple or glue the ends where they meet.

8 REPEAT ON THE OTHER THREE SIDES.

9 TAKE TWO MORE RED STRIPS and two more green strips. Put them in to pairs (it's up to you whether you mix your colours or keep like with like). Attach one end of one pair of strips to a corner (top of the fan) and cross it over the centre of the basket and attach to the opposite corner.

10 TAKE THE REMAINING PAIR OF STRIPS and repeat step 11 using the other two corners of the basket.

11 YOU CAN LEAVE YOUR HANDLE PLAIN or you might like to make a paper bow to attach to it as a decoration. These attractive baskets look fabulous filled with brightly wrapped sweets.

DID YOU KNOW? If you imagine that practically any container or packaging that is now made from plastic, cardboard or plywood would once have been made of basketry, it gives you an idea of the importance of basket makers throughout history.

Photography

✦

If you want to cover your bedroom notice-board with fun photos of all your best mates, you don't have to rely on a photo-booth. But for the best photo collages, you need to know how to take a good picture and, most importantly, how to look good on film.

Taking a gorgeous photo

It doesn't much matter whether you're using a film, disposable or digital camera, the rules for taking a decent photograph remain the same.

YOU WILL NEED
- A camera
- Film (unless camera is digital)
- Batteries
- Friends to photograph

STEPS

1 MAKE SURE THE BATTERIES in your camera are fully charged and you've got plenty of film (if you're using a film camera). Then you're ready to start.

2 CHOOSE THE LOCATION for your photo-shoot and get your volunteer(s) into comfortable positions. Pick a background that fits the kind of photos you want to take – perhaps a park or back yard for sunny photos, an old building for grungy pics or a cosy room if you want your models to look sultry.

3 WHEN LOOKING THROUGH THE VIEWFINDER or at the screen, make sure the head of your model is near the top of the photo, and that she fills the whole shot. If the head is in the centre of your picture, you'll have a lot of sky or ceiling in your finished photo.

4 MAKE SURE EVERYONE IS RELAXED. If your models are tense, you'll see it in the photo. So keep chatting away to them to put them at their ease.

5 LOOK OVER THE CAMERA AT YOUR MODELS just as you press the shutter so that they are looking at a person, not a gadget – it gives a better result.

6 TRY TO ARRANGE THE GROUP so that their hands and feet are not in the foreground – perspective makes the things nearest the camera look biggest. If they're sitting down, get your models to tuck their feet back rather than stretching their legs out towards the camera.

7 USE A FLASH WHEN THERE IS LITTLE DAYLIGHT or you are in a dark room, or your models will just come out as blurry shadows. If there's enough natural light, then avoid using the flash because it bleaches out the atmosphere.

8 DON'T TAKE PHOTOGRAPHS with the sun (or any strong light source) directly behind your models, or your pictures will come out as silhouettes. Try to get the sun behind you or to one side.

9 IF YOUR MODELS ARE STANDING in the shade against a bright background, try using the flash to even out the light levels – otherwise the picture will either have your models looking shadowy, or the background overexposed (so it comes out as a white blur).

10 EVEN IF YOU THINK YOU'VE GOT A CRACKING SHOT, always take a couple of photos in each pose (although this isn't so necessary with a digital camera where you can see the results immediately).

11 KEEP SNAPPING AWAY and you're bound to get some great shots as well as having lots of fun.

DID YOU KNOW? If you have a digital camera, you can now take the memory card in to a photo-developing lab and they will download all or selected images and print them for you.

Looking good in a photo

Being photogenic is a real blessing, but anyone can improve how good they look on film with a few simple insider tricks of the trade from those in the modelling business.

YOU WILL NEED

- A photographer
- Self-confidence!

STEPS

1 DON'T STAND STRAIGHT IN FRONT OF THE CAMERA – angle your body slightly and turn your head to look into the lens – much more flattering.

2 TIP YOUR HEAD and find what angles work best for your face – it's true that everyone has a best side!

3 TRY EXPERIMENTING WITH TILTING YOUR HEAD down very slightly but don't overdo it – this simply gives you double chins in the photo.

4 YOU WANT THE LIGHT SHINING ON YOU from the front or the side: definitely not from above or below, unless you want to look like an extra in a horror film.

5 MAKE EYE CONTACT with the camera and imagine that it's someone you really like – this translates on to the film.

6 REMEMBER TO SMILE. Trying to look sultry is fine for models but for us lesser mortals it usually ends up with us simply looking miserable.

7 IF IT'S A SERIES OF PHOTOS IN THE SAME POSE (official photographers can take ages), look away and back to camera just before the shutter for full eyes and to avoid a glazed look, and also relax the smile between shots to avoid a fixed grimace.

8 AND REMEMBER, anything that is less than flattering can be consigned to the bin, because everyone has their off days.

Homemade paper

With the advent of text messaging, the art of letter writing is all but dead. That's why it's such a lovely surprise to receive a hand-written note from a friend – and if it's on gorgeous handmade paper too, then so much the better.

YOU WILL NEED

- Scrap paper (anything from old magazines and cards to tissue paper, napkins and typing paper)
- A sponge
- A wooden frame (you can use an old picture frame if you like)
- A piece of fine metal mesh, the kind used for window screening (available from hardware stores or from craft shops)
- A plastic bowl (large enough to totally submerge your frame)
- Food processor/blender
- White felt or flannel fabric squares
- Tacks or large staples (to attach screen to frame)
- Liquid starch

STEPS

1 CHOOSE YOUR PIECES OF PAPER FOR RECYCLING. You can either stick to one type, or mix and match if you like.

2 TEAR THE PAPER INTO SMALL PIECES and put it in the blender (don't over fill it – about halfway is fine). Now fill the blender with warm water. Run it on slow, and then increase the speed for about 30–40 seconds to make a smooth pulp, without any flakes.

3 STRETCH YOUR SCREEN MATERIAL over the wooden frame and staple it in place. It should be as tight as possible.

③

4 HALF FILL YOUR PLASTIC BOWL WITH WATER. Add about three blender-loads of pulp to the water (the more you add, the thicker your finished paper will be). Stir the mixture.

5 ADD TWO TEASPOONS OF LIQUID STARCH to the pulp. This helps to prevent the ink from spreading on the paper. Now you're ready to start making the sheets.

6 SUBMERGE THE FRAME IN THE PULP MIXTURE. Make sure it is level, then gently shake it from side to side in the mixture so that the pulp on top of the screen forms an even layer.

7 CAREFULLY LIFT THE MOULD UP AND OUT OF THE WATER. Hold it there to allow most of the water to drain through the screen.

8 FROM THIS FIRST ATTEMPT, you can gauge whether the pulp mixture is too thick or too thin – too thick and your pulp layer will be lumpy and uneven; too thin and you won't get enough pulp to make a sheet.

9 ADJUST THE THICKNESS OF THE MIXTURE by adding more pulp or scooping some out of the bowl with your mould.

10 ONCE YOU'RE HAPPY WITH THE MIXTURE, repeat step 7 to make your first sheet of paper. Hold the mould over the bowl until it stops dripping. Then gently place one edge of the mould on the side of your felt or flannel square.

11 CAREFULLY LAY THE MOULD down flat so the paper is directly on the fabric. Use the sponge to press out as much excess water as possible. (You can wring the sponge out into the plastic bowl – waste not, want not!)

12 PAY ATTENTION NOW, because the next bit is tricky! While holding the fabric square flat, carefully lift the edge of the mould. With any luck, the wet sheet of paper will remain on the fabric. Has it stuck? Perhaps you haven't pressed out enough water, in which case you'll have to try again. Don't worry, you'll soon get the hang of it.

13 REPEAT THE ABOVE STEPS, stacking your fabric squares and paper on top of each other on a baking tray (you'll see why in a minute).

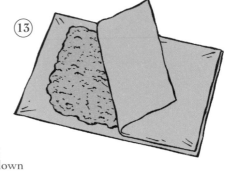

14 PLACE A FABRIC SQUARE on top of the last pair in the stack. Take a second baking sheet and, moving the pile to a sink or bath, squeeze down to press any remaining water out of the stack.

15 NOW, GENTLY SEPARATE THE SHEETS, which can then be dried either by hanging them on a clothesline or by laying them out on sheets of newspaper.

16 ONCE THEY'RE DRY, you can peel them off the fabric and you have your very own beautiful and unique writing paper.

17 YOU CAN ADD ANYTHING TO THE PULP MIXTURE after it's been through the blender, to customise your finished sheets – seeds, petals, tin foil, pieces of yarn – let your imagination run riot!

DID YOU KNOW? The word 'paper' comes from the word 'papyrus', which is the name of a type of reed. The pith of this reed was used by the Ancient Egyptians to make a paper-like substance for writing on as long ago as 2600 B.C. It wasn't until 105 A.D. in China that Ts'ai Lun invented paper as we know it today by mixing hemp, bark and linen with water, mashing it to a pulp and then pressing out the liquid.

Gardening

❦❦

Contrary to popular myth, you do not have to be a senior citizen to enjoy gardening. In fact, you'd be amazed how many top celebrities cite gardening as a way of relaxing. Perhaps you haven't caught the gardening bug yet, but you will.

Growing a sunflower

A good place to start for those of you who want to become a green-fingered goddess is by planting something tough like a sunflower.

YOU WILL NEED
- A garden trowel
- Sunflower seeds (available from garden centres and supermarkets)
- A watering can
- A garden spade

STEPS

1 IN SPRING, after the danger of frost has passed, find a clear flowerbed in a nice, sunny spot and loosen the soil with a trowel. Then plant your seeds 10–15 cm (4–6 inches) apart and cover them with 12 mm (½ an inch) of soil.

2 WATER THEM JUST ENOUGH to keep the soil moist – don't overwater them or they won't grow. Keep watering them as the seeds sprout and your miniature sunflower plants start to develop. Check the soil once or twice a week to make sure it's not bone dry. Your plants should soon start to shoot up into tall, straight stems with large, flat leaves.

3 EXPECT THE FLOWERS TO DEVELOP IN THE LATE SUMMER and early autumn. As the flowers start to fade, cut the dead heads off to encourage new flowers to grow in their place.

4 IF YOUR VARIETY IS AN ANNUAL (i.e. has a lifespan of just one year), pull the plants out and discard them in the autumn, once the frost has gotten to them. If you chose a perennial variety (i.e. one that blooms each year) then just cut them down and wait until next year for them to flower again!

5 YOU CAN GIVE YOUR SUNFLOWER A HEAD START during a cold spring by planting the seed in a little pot on your windowsill, and letting it grow into a seedling indoors. Then you can plant out the seedling rather than seeds. Don't forget to water your little pot regularly, or your seedlings won't get started!

Growing herbs

For the more experienced gardeners among you, have you thought about growing a herb garden? Not only does it look very pretty, but the herbs you grow can be used in the kitchen too.

YOU WILL NEED

- Containers of various sizes
- Your choice of herb plants in pots (available from garden centres)
- Good multi-purpose compost
- A trowel
- Imagination

STEPS

1 MAKE SURE ALL OF YOUR CHOSEN CONTAINERS have good drainage. If you're using plastic pots, you can carefully poke a hole in the bottom with an awl or a screwdriver.

2 FILL THEM THREE-QUARTERS FULL with compost.

3 WHEN CHOOSING YOUR HERBS, think about what may be used for cooking in your household – do you like mint and basil, or maybe rosemary and thyme?

4 DON'T FORGET TO CHECK the labels to see how big the plants can grow. Did you know angelica can grow to over 1.8 m (6 feet) tall, for example? Make sure your garden won't get so big it takes over the whole kitchen!

WARNING

Mint is an invasive herb. If you plant it in the garden, a clump is likely to pop up in the middle of your lawn or among your daffodils, so it is best planted in a small container on its own and either left free-standing or sunk into the earth of the garden.

5 ALLOCATE HERBS TO EACH POT according to how big the plants grow, and how likely you are to use them in your cooking. For example, you could put French lavender in the largest pot, basil or coriander in the next size down, then marjoram or oregano in the next smallest, mint in another and finally trailing thyme in the smallest.

6 Tip the seedlings out of their little pots and plant them out in your containers. Surround them with more compost, press them down a little to make sure they're secure (but not so much that the soil is packed together) and give them a little water.

7 THEN ARRANGE YOUR POTS ATTRACTIVELY on a windowsill where they will get plenty of sunlight, and watch them grow!

8 IF YOU'RE PUSHED FOR SPACE, you can grow herbs in strawberry pots with something large like lavender and chives in the main part and other herbs in the side holes. Or you can even plant them out in hanging baskets.

9 YOU MUST MAKE SURE YOUR CONTAINERS ARE WELL-WATERED because the herbs tend to dry out more quickly than if they were planted in the garden.

Your own jewellery

✦✦✦

A girl can never have too much jewellery but if ready cash is in
short supply, making your own can be a fun and cost-effective
solution. And what's more, you get to design and create
something beautiful and unique. All the bits and pieces listed
below should be available cheaply from craft stores or on-line.

Of course, designing jewellery is big business in the fashion industry, with famous
names like Lacroix and Dolce & Gabbana releasing their own ranges. Start
working on your own designs, and who knows where you might end up?

Dangle earrings

YOU WILL NEED

- Beads – choose coloured or glass
  beads that compliment each other
  and which you find appealing
- 5-cm (2-inch) headpins (a straight
  wire with a flat head on one end,
  used to make bead dangles)
- Ear wires
- Spacers
- Silver metal beads
- Round-nose pliers (used for
  making loops)
- Chain-nose pliers (these have
  straight and smooth jaws. They're
  designed to grasp and hold the
  wire without leaving marks)
- Wire cutters

STEPS

1 ARRANGE YOUR BEADS ON THE HEAD PINS, using spacers between each bead.
You can have great fun choosing the colours and sizes but make sure you do
both earrings at the same time so that you get the order and sizes balanced.

2 USING THE TIP OF THE ROUND-NOSE PLIERS held against the top bead, bend the
head pin wire to 90 degrees.

3 READJUST THE POSITION OF YOUR PLIERS so you can now fold the wire around the tip of the round nose to make a loop.

4 HOLD THE LOOP WITH THE PLIERS in your dominant hand, and with your other hand wrap the wire snugly around the top of the line of beads.

5 USING THE WIRE CUTTERS, clip the end of the wire very close to the wrap, so that your loop is as neat and tight as possible.

6 IF THE CUT END OF THE WIRE IS SHARP use the tip of the chain-nose pliers to press it down so it doesn't stick out. You should now have a string of beads with a small wire loop at the top.

7 AGAIN USING THE PLIERS, open the loop on the ear wires. Use a sideways movement to do this, rather than just pulling the loop apart, which can weaken the wire.

8 SLIDE THE LOOP YOU MADE at the top of your dangle onto the open loop of the ear wire. (10)

9 RE-CLOSE THE LOOP in the ear wire using the pliers.

10 AND THERE YOU ARE – a beautiful pair of unique earrings made by and exclusive to you! Just wait though – all your friends will soon be asking you to make earrings for them too.

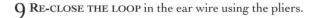

DID YOU KNOW? Since civilisation began, jewellery has adorned important men and women. In fact, magnificent bracelets, pendants, necklaces, rings, armlets, earrings and head ornaments have been found in burial sites dating back to ancient Egypt in 3000 B.C. Today we might think of earrings as being worn by women, but in fact the oldest known depiction of them is on men – soldiers in the army of ancient Persia, in fact, from a wall-carving in Persepolis dated to the sixth century B.C.

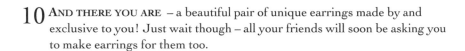

A leather and bead necklace

YOU WILL NEED

- 48-cm (19-inch) length of leather thong, 3 mm (⅛ in) thick
- 7.5–12.5 cm (3–5 inches) of beads – use long and round beads but remember, they must have a hole large enough to fit over the leather
- A commercial clasp
- A crimp-style or clam shell connector
- 10 cm (4 inches) of 20-gauge wire, the same colour as your clasp
- A flush cutter
- Round-nose pliers
- Chain-nose pliers

STEPS

1 AT ONE END OF THE LEATHER, lay the connector. Wrap the leather around the loop in the connector and then, using your chain-nose pliers, squeeze both sides of the connector over the leather to grasp it firmly. Cut off any excess leather close to the connector.

2 NOW WITH ONE END FIXED WITH A CONNECTOR, have fun stringing your combination of beads onto the leather. You need about 7.5-12.5 cm (3–5 inches) of beads.

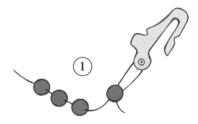

3 ONCE YOU HAVE COMPLETED STRINGING YOUR BEADS, add the clasp to the other end of the leather following step 1 above. And hey presto! A beautiful leather and bead necklace that can be worn at any time.

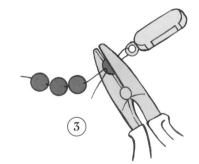

A comic strip

If you're good at drawing, you can keep yourself and your friends amused by creating a comic strip.

YOU WILL NEED
- A pencil, pen and/or a slim black marker
- Paper
- Imagination

STEPS

1 EXPERIMENT WITH DRAWING SOME CHARACTERS. These can be human, aliens, animals or objects that come to life – whatever you fancy. Then think about their characters and possible names.

2 THINK OF A SHORT, HUMOROUS TALE or a joke and mentally break it into sections. Now create a rough image for each section and quickly sketch it down, using stick figures or quick drawings.

3 THINK OF A TITLE AND CAPTIONS, if any – a comic strip can be a purely visual joke if you prefer.

4 NOW DRAW YOUR GOOD COPY, with characters drawn in full and all details and colour added. Then show the final version to your friends and see if it makes them laugh!

5 ALWAYS KEEP YOUR COMIC STRIPS in an album or portfolio. Who knows, one day you may get them published!

DID YOU KNOW? Richard Outcault is credited with creating the first comic strip in 1895, called *Yellow Kid*. Although comic strips and books were published before this, Outcault was the first artist to use the balloon – an outlined space where what the characters said was written down.

A play

✦

Can you imagine how thrilling it would be to see a play that you had written performed on Broadway or in the West End of London? Well, even Shakespeare himself had to start somewhere. So, no time like the present – let's get creative!

YOU WILL NEED

- A computer or pen and paper
- Imagination

STEPS

1 FIRSTLY, YOU MUST THINK UP THE THEME and story-line for your play. Then think up a title and head the page with it.

2 NEXT, LIST THE CAST in order of appearance. Put a brief description next to each character's name to help your actors get to know their parts.

3 START WITH SCENE ONE and briefly describe the setting. Is it inside or out? Are there props or scenery that will be important later, and if so where should they be positioned?

4 ON THE LEFT-HAND SIDE OF THE PAGE, print the character's name and then, indented, you write the character's words. There is no need to use speech marks.

5 FOR EACH NEW SPEAKER, you start a new line – again, putting their name on the left and their speech indented.

6 USE STAGE DIRECTIONS, written in the present tense, to describe the speech or the actions.

7 CONTINUE TO WRITE EACH SCENE in this way until your play is complete. Then get some friends together and start rehearsing!

Pressing flowers

— ❖ —

Whether you use them for making homemade greetings cards
(see pages 42–43) or for displays, pressed flowers can be as
beautiful as the fresh variety. And what's more, they last forever.
Flower pressing is great fun to do, and it's very simple.

YOU WILL NEED

- A selection of your favourite
  flowers or foliage, picked and
  ready to go

- A heavy book such as a phone
  directory or dictionary
- A sheet of newspaper

STEPS

1 PLACE YOUR PICKED FLOWERS and foliage in the fridge to keep fresh while you
prepare your press.

2 ARRANGE THE FLOWERS on one half of the sheet of newspaper, being careful to
make sure that the leaves and petals do not overlap. Then fold the top half of the
newspaper sheet down over the flowers. Some flowers are better suited to being
pressed than others, so it's worth experimenting a bit before planning to use
them in any artwork.

3 OPEN THE HEAVIEST BOOK in the middle and place the newspaper on the open
page. Close the book and place the other books or heavy objects on top.

4 AFTER ABOUT THREE DAYS, open the book and carefully remove the pressed
flowers from the newspaper. They're now ready to use in an arrangement, on a
card, as artwork or in whichever way you choose.

Rubbing leaves

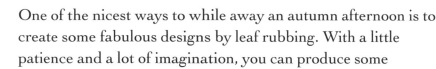

One of the nicest ways to while away an autumn afternoon is to create some fabulous designs by leaf rubbing. With a little patience and a lot of imagination, you can produce some gorgeous nature-themed patterns.

YOU WILL NEED
- 2 sheets of plain white paper
- A collection of autumn leaves
- A packet of coloured crayons

STEPS

1 Collect a selection of autumn leaves in different shapes and sizes. Place the leaves, vein side up, on a sheet of white paper in any pattern you like, and put the second sheet of white paper on top of your design.

2 Take off any paper wrapping around your crayons. Using the long side of a crayon rather than the tip, rub gently over the sheet. The outline of your leaves will appear as if by magic and reveal your beautiful design!

3 We tend instinctively to turn to autumnal shades of browns, russets and greens when leaf rubbing but you can actually use any colour, however vibrant, in your design. Go crazy and see what works for you!

Room decorating

❧❧

Sick to death of your bedroom? Is it still decorated from when
you were in your Fairy Princess period? Then your room is
soooo ready for a change, and here are some tips for jazzing it up
without it costing you (or your parents) a fortune.

YOU WILL NEED
- Some spare cash
- Imagination
- A ruthless streak (for throwing
  away things you really don't need
  any more)

STEPS

1 FIRST, DECIDE WHAT SORT OF LOOK OR STYLE you want before you get started.
Do you want bright and cheerful, open plan and airy, or dark and mysterious?
Check out some magazines and the Internet for great ideas and inspiration –
they're particularly useful on colour schemes. And work out a rough budget
before you start so you can match the scale of your plans to your savings.

2 CHANGING CARPETS AND CURTAINS ISN'T EASY, so try to choose a colour scheme
that will compliment them rather than clash.

3 PAINTING THE WALLS is the first step for a completely new look – for example,
pastel shades are great for making a small room look bigger. If you can't stretch
to buying cans of paint, see if your family has some old tins leftover from
previous decorations that are a cool colour. Don't worry if you can't manage a
repaint, there are plenty of other ways to revamp your room.

4 NEW BEDDING AND CURTAINS can make a huge difference. If buying new ones
is going to break the bank, what about a new throw on the bed or some new
scatter cushions? Buy a cheap, colourful length of material and fix it up over
your old curtains – it'll look great, and you can still draw the curtains behind it
to keep out the light while you're getting your beauty sleep. And if you can't
stand the carpet, cover it up with a nice throw or rug.

5 CHOOSE SOME POSTERS. It doesn't have to be of your favourite band or hot hunk. It could be something arty – your favourite museum is the best place for these – or something retro. What about a moody black and white poster of Audrey Hepburn, for example?

6 DE-CLUTTER – GET RID OF ALL THE JUNK that's accumulated over the years that you never use. Put any toys that you really can't bear to part with in a bag in the attic. You can always keep a few stuffed toys on a shelf, in a chair or on your bed, but moderation is key here.

7 IF YOU HAVEN'T GOT A MIRROR, GET ONE. And if you're tired of the one you have, rejuvenate it by painting the frame, or sticking on shells, baubles or fake gems.

8 SOMEWHERE TO SIT immediately transforms a girl's room into a hangout. A funky armchair is ideal – you can even get inflatable ones now – or what about a beanbag?

9 WORK ON THE LIGHTING – a desk lamp is essential for your working area, and a glitzy shade for the overhead light will transform the room.

10 FINALLY, TIME TO PERSONALISE. Flick through your albums and find your favourite photos of your best friends, your pets and your family. Then make a collage of them on a notice board or in a clip-frame, and adorn your walls with happy smiley faces!

Personalised greetings cards

❖ ❖

You can buy some really cute cards for just about every occasion now in the shops, but if you really want to tailor a greetings card for a special event (or a special person), then the best way is to make your own card and put a personal message inside.

YOU WILL NEED

- Thick, good quality coloured paper or greetings card paper (available from craft shops)
- Tracing paper
- Rubber stamps and ink pads
- Glue or double-sided sticky tape
- Felt pens, glitter, pressed flowers or other colourful decorations
- Scissors
- Thinner coloured paper

STEPS

1 TAKE A SHEET OF COLOURED CARD and fold it in half to make basic greetings card. Make sure the corners line up before you fold, so that your card doesn't look lop-sided.

2 FIND A SIMPLE SHAPE that you like and that will appeal to the person who'll be getting the card. Perhaps the outline of a cat, or a star. You can find images on the Internet, or around the house – you can even take them from pastry cutters.

3 TRACE THE SHAPE and transfer it on to some coloured card or stiff paper. Make three copies. Cut them out, decorate them with felt pen or glitter and then put to one side.

4 USE FELT PENS OR WIGGLY STRIPS of coloured paper to make a background for your card – try and make it look like streamers rather than spaghetti!

5 NEXT, ATTACH THE THREE CUT-OUT SHAPES to the card using glue or double-sided sticky tape. If you can't find a shape you like, try using pressed flowers.

6 USING A SMALL STAMP, and ink in different colours, scatter stamped shapes in the spaces between the design. These can be smaller versions of your cut-out shapes, or something completely different.

7 CHOOSE A FABULOUS FONT in a word-processing programme on your computer. Type and print out a personal message to your friend, then trace it on to your card very lightly. Now draw the final lettering with a colourful, bold felt pen. Now you have a personalised card for any occasion, bound to cheer up whoever is lucky enough to receive it!

Wrapping paper

Why not continue the theme by personalising the wrapping paper for a gift to accompany your personalised card? Wrap your gift in plain brown or white paper, then either cut out a few more star shapes to match the card and stick on, or using the stencilled lettering that you used inside the card (particularly if it includes your friend's name), trace this over the paper and go over it in bright felt pen.

DID YOU KNOW? The custom of sending shop-bought Christmas cards originated in London in 1843. Prior to that, people gave each other handwritten holiday greetings, first in person and then by post.

Chapter Two

Adventuring

WE GIRLS MIGHT ENJOY getting glammed up and looking our best, but we also enjoy a bit of adventure in our lives. And what better way to seek thrills than to get out into the great outdoors and have some fun?

✦

Whether it's exploring on foot or horseback, sleeping under the stars, making your own shelter or toasting marshmallows over an open fire that you made and lit yourself – if you're ready for some adventure, then the following pages are for you.

✦

And if the weather means you have to curb your outdoor exploration, never fear – we've got plenty of adventures that can be experienced from the comfort of your own home, such as sending secret messages and becoming a detective. What are you waiting for? Read on.

Trotting on a horse

✦✦✦

There was a time when riding a horse was about the only way to get around. Now we use planes, trains and automobiles, but horse-riding remains a sport enjoyed by many people around the world. And it's us girls who love riding the most – three-quarters of all regular riders are female.

The building block of all horse-riding skills is to be able to get your horse to trot. So let's get in the saddle and get out on the open plains.

YOU WILL NEED
- A horse (saddled and bridled)
- An open space in which to ride
- A hard hat

Rising trot

Once your horse is walking comfortably, you can ask him to trot by squeezing gently with your lower legs. You need to squeeze a bit harder than you would to keep him walking forward – you might even have to give him a gentle kick with your heels.

When trotting, the horse moves its legs in diagonal pairs – it lifts its left front (near fore) and right back (off hind) legs together, followed by the opposite pair. You will feel the horse's body swaying from side to side as each hind leg is lifted.

Keeping your hands still, you rise to the post in rhythm with your horse's movement. Sounds confusing? Well, try to imagine that each time one pair of the horse's legs lands on the ground, you sit in the saddle, and as the other pair of legs lands on the ground, you rise slightly out of the saddle, pushing your hips forward (it should be more of a gentle push forwards rather than aiming for height!) As soon as your seat is back in the saddle, it should be on its way up again in a flowing, continuous movement.

At first it can be difficult to keep up with the rhythm but it helps to listen to the beat of your horse's hooves on the ground and count one-two-one-two in time to the beats, sitting and rising at the appropriate time. A little practice and you'll soon have it.

Sitting trot

A sitting trot might seem like the easy option but it can actually be quite uncomfortable for both the horse and rider if you don't get it right. So start as you did with the rising trot by urging your horse on with your legs. Try to stay relaxed with your back loose and legs comfortable. In this way, the trot will feel less bouncy. Remember to take deep, slow breaths and relax – if you get nervous and cling on tightly to minimise the bouncing around, your tensed legs will make your horse think that you want him to go faster, which is not what you want at all.

> **WARNING**
>
> Horse-riding is a high-risk sport. Horses are unpredictable animals and accidents can happen, so make sure you get proper tuition if you're new to the sport. And please always wear a riding hat!

DID YOU KNOW? Horses and ponies are measured at the shoulder in hands. A hand is equivalent to 10 cm (4 inches). Anything less than 14.2 hands is classed as a pony. Horses cannot vomit. Nor can they breathe through their mouths, so you'll never see a horse panting like a dog.

Flying a kite

❖

On a bright gusty day, no girl wants to be cooped up indoors. But, instead of just going for a walk, why not dig out your old kite and have some fun? There's nothing like feeling the live pull of a kite on the end of a string – it's almost like having a pet bird (only cheaper to feed!)

YOU WILL NEED
- A kite
- A moderately windy day (too gusty and you'll lose your kite)

STEPS

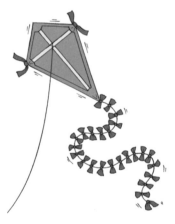

1 FIND A LARGE OPEN AREA free of trees and power lines.

2 LET OUT A SMALL LENGTH OF KITE STRING and, holding the string in your hand, run with the kite behind you into the wind until it lifts it.

3 KEEP LETTING OUT STRING until the kite reaches a good height.

4 KEEP AN EYE ON YOUR KITE, in case the wind drops. Run into the wind or pull on the string to give your kite some extra lift.

5 BRING THE KITE DOWN by slowly winding the kite string around the kite spool, and catch it just before it hits the ground to avoid damaging it.

WARNING

Stay away from electrical lines. If your kite becomes entangled, leave it there. Never fly your kite during a thunderstorm.

Exploring

❦ ❦

There's no greater sense of freedom than setting off on a day's
adventure with your friends, armed only with a packed lunch and
a map (oh, and you'd better pack your mobile phone in case of
emergencies – or just in case you fancy a chat!) But before you
head off into the wild blue yonder, there are a few basic skills that
you should get under your belt.

Reading a map

The basic tools for finding where you are and where you're going are a map and a
compass. You can pick up a local map from tourist centres or park stations. Check
the scale on the map when you plan your route – a 1:50,000 map scale means the
map area is 50,000 times smaller than the real area, so a distance of 2.5 cm (1 inch)
on the map is 125,000 cm(50,000 inches) or about 1.25 km (0.8 miles).

YOU WILL NEED
- A full colour map
- A compass

STEPS

1 FIND THE TWO POINTS ON THE MAP that you want to travel between. Line up
your compass edge between the two points, so that your direction-of-travel
arrow is pointing to your destination.

2 ROTATE THE COMPASS HOUSING until the orienting lines in the centre are
pointing to the top of your map. (You can do this by lining them up parallel to
the grid lines.)

3 NOW ROTATE THE DIAL until the north pointer lines up with the mark on the
dial that joins the direction of travel arrow (this is called the index line).

4 NOW READ THE BEARING at the bottom of the direction-of-travel arrow, at the index line. Remember that you need to take into account the difference between grid north (on your map) and magnetic north (on your compass). This is called magnetic variation and your map should tell you how many degrees to add to your bearing.

5 TO HEAD IN THE RIGHT DIRECTION, you must now re-orientate your compass. This means turning the whole compass around until the magnetic north needle points in the same direction as the orienting arrow. The way the direction-of-travel arrow is now pointing is the direction you must walk in to get to your destination.

Don't forget to take regular bearings during your journey if you want to stay on track. Rather than struggling with an open map the size of a small sail that's likely to blow away in a high wind, always fold your map into a manageable size with your route clearly in view.

DID YOU KNOW? Contour lines on a map are a way of showing you how high the land is. They join together places of the same height and form patterns that help us to imagine what the land actually looks like. Remember that the closer together the contour lines are, the steeper the land. Contour lines that are wide apart show us that the land is flatter.

Happy hiking

So, now you know which direction you're going in but do you know how to get to your destination without blisters and still in high spirits? Well, here are a few tips on happy hiking. You need to be prepared for changeable weather conditions, so a backpack with an extra layer and some waterproof clothing is essential. You should also be able to find your way back home so make sure you familiarise yourself with map reading before you set out on your adventure.

YOU WILL NEED

- Walking shoes or hiking boots
- Outdoor clothing

TIPS

1 DON'T WEAR BRAND NEW FOOTWEAR on a hike or you'll end up with blisters. Wear your shoes around town until they're comfortable, and then start with short, easy hikes to get your muscles used to walking longer distances.

2 CHOOSE GOOD WEATHER to start hiking because it gives you a better idea of what's involved without having to contend with wind and rain.

3 IT'S A GOOD IDEA AT FIRST TO GO WITH experienced hikers. If you don't have any hiking friends or family, join an organised group until you've got the hang of things – the local library is a good place to find details.

4 ALWAYS WEAR COMFORTABLE CLOTHES that are designed for the job. And don't worry that you'll look like a dork – there's some really great-looking outdoor gear available now. Take water and high-energy snacks with you. And don't forget the warm gear in winter and a hat or sun-block in summer.

5 ONCE YOU HAVE SOME GROUP HIKING EXPERIENCE under your belt, you can start to go for longer and more challenging hikes.

WARNING

Always make sure someone responsible knows where you're going and when you expect to be back – even the best explorers sometimes get lost.

Finding water

It may not be quite on the scale of Dr Livingstone locating the source of the Nile, but finding water can be a fun challenge, even in your own neighbourhood. It can also save you carting around tons of the stuff for washing and cooking when you're out camping. If you're careful about making sure it's pure and free of germs, you can even drink it.

Tracking down water sources

There are some surefire practical ways to find water in the wild that humans have been using since the Stone Age.

YOU WILL NEED
- Thirst
- Somewhere to explore

STEPS

1 LOOK IN VALLEY BOTTOMS FOR STREAMS. Dig in dry streambeds; the water may be just below the surface.

2 AT THE COAST, LOOK FOR PLANTS growing in faults on cliffsides – you may find a spring.

3 PLANTS LIKE BAMBOO OFTEN TRAP WATER in cavities in their stems. Cut the stem open to find water inside. Don't forget to strain it – you don't want dead flies slipping down!

4 TIE CLEAN CLOTHS AROUND YOUR LEGS and ankles and walk through wet vegetation (particularly in the morning when plants are covered in dew). These cloths can then be wrung out into a container.

Divining

For thousands of years, people have claimed to be able to find water using a Y-shaped stick held in front of them. As they pass over an underground water source, the stick starts to twitch and vibrate. This technique is known as divining and, who knows, you may just have the gift.

YOU WILL NEED
- A Y-shaped stick (preferably willow)
- A spade

STEPS

1 HOLD EACH END of the 'Y' part of the stick and point the tip out in front of you. Hold it roughly parallel to the ground or pointing slightly down.

2 WALK SLOWLY and empty your mind of clutter and buzz.

3 IF THE STICK STARTS TO TWITCH or pull towards the ground, there may be water underground. Time to get out your spade and start digging!

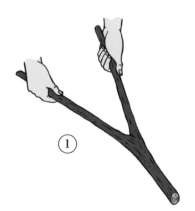

DID YOU KNOW? If you run out of food, you can keep going for several days, even weeks without eating. Water is much more important – an adult can survive only three days without it.

Collecting water

❧ ❧

If you still can't find any water, you can always collect it for yourself during a storm or rainshower.

YOU WILL NEED

- Plastic sheeting
- 2 long, straight sticks
- 2 shorter sticks
- String

- A collecting pot
- A heavy stone
- A trowel (optional)

STEPS

1 LAY YOUR PLASTIC SHEETING on the ground and mark out the points where the corners lie.

2 PUSH TWO TWO LONG STICKS INTO THE GROUND at the back corners (using a trowel if necessary to loosen the ground) and two shorter sticks at the front corners. Drape the sheeting over the sticks so it sits off the ground and forms a slope from the tall sticks down to the short sticks.

3 POKE A SMALL HOLE in the middle of the sheeting at the lower end. Tie a piece of string to this hole and tuck the other end under a heavy stone on the ground beneath. This pulls the middle of the front of the sheet down to make a sort of spout, down which the collected rainwater will run.

4 PUT A CONTAINER UNDER THIS SPOUT and, hey presto, as soon as it rains, you'll have cold running water.

WARNING

Always boil water that you collect before drinking it — water that looks clean can still carry some invisible but very nasty bugs. You can boil it over your own open fire (see pages 55-57).

Making a campfire and cooking on it

If you can light a fire anywhere under any conditions, then you'll always have a source of warmth and protection and a means of cooking and signalling. It can be useful, even life-saving, if you're ever stranded in the wild, but it's also cool and exciting when you're out camping.

Making a wigwam fire

This basic fire setup (or 'lay' as a professional would call it) is easy to build, and almost guaranteed to be easy to light.

YOU WILL NEED

- Tinder (dry grass, dead leaves, crumbled-up bark)
- Kindling (twigs, small sticks and small, dry leaves)
- Medium-sized sticks
- Logs
- Matches

STEPS

1 CLEAR AN AREA OF LEAVES, twigs, dry grass – anything flammable – until you've got a bare earth surface.

2 MAKE A SMALL PILE OF DRY KINDLING – little sticks that will start to burn quickly. About pencil-size is good. It has to be dry, though, or you won't get anywhere.

WARNING

The golden rule of fire-making is only burn what you want to burn. Be very careful that the fire cannot spread to your tent, or surrounding wood or vegetation. If your clothes catch fire, immediately stop what you're doing, drop to the ground and roll over and over to smother the flames.

3 AROUND THE KINDLING, build a wigwam with thin but longer sticks.

4 PUT A BALL OF TINDER INSIDE THE KINDLING – this is what you use to start the fire, so it can be made from anything that will catch light easily. Light the tinder with a match. The kindling will soon catch, and in turn set fire to the outer layer of sticks.

5 ONCE YOUR FIRE IS LIT, it will burn fiercely. The wigwam will collapse into a pile of hot, burning embers. Now, very carefully, add more sticks and keep feeding the fire till it's big enough to keep you warm.

6 WHEN IT'S WINDY, your fire can blow out before it gets started, or burn so fiercely you use up all your firewood right away. In these conditions, dig a trench and light your fire in it. Or encircle your fire with rocks to save fuel.

Cooking outdoors

When camping out, you use the fire to boil water, and then let the flames die down and use the embers and hot ash for cooking. The embers don't burn so fiercely, so they'll cook your meal evenly all the way through. Trying to cook on flames will turn your food into a blackened mess on the outside, and leave it raw in the middle! Always make sure your food is properly cooked before eating it.

Some foods such as fish can be cooked directly in the embers of a fire, wrapped in foil to stop them burning. Otherwise you can use sharpened sticks for a skewer (ideal for vegetable kebabs) or as a toasting fork (good for sausages, toast and marshmallows). If you're lucky enough to have a pot or billycan, here's how to make a pot rest so you can cook a proper meal.

YOU WILL NEED
- 2 sturdy forked sticks
- A longer, straight stick, also reasonably strong
- A pot
- An open fire
- Ingredients (see below)

STEPS

1 DRIVE THE BASE OF A STURDY, FORKED STICK into the ground near the fire, and another one on the opposite side of the fire.

2 REST A LONGER STICK across the two forks so it rests over the fire. The trick is to get the forked sticks long enough so that your crosspiece doesn't catch light!

3 HANG YOUR CAN from the crosspiece so it sits close to the heat of the embers. Now you're ready to start cooking.

4 ADD WHATEVER INGREDIENTS you like to your pot. For a one-pot delight, add chopped vegetables, some meat, a stock cube and some water and leave it to stew. If you can't face all the peeling and chopping, simply drop a boil-in-the-bag dinner into some boiling water. *Bon appetit!*

WARNING

Make sure all your food is cooked thoroughly. Eating raw food, especially meat, can make you very ill.

Putting out a fire safely

Unless watched at all times, fires can spread easily and become dangerous. When you're ready to put the fire out, make sure it's thoroughly extinguished, so you don't put yourselves or anyone else at risk.

Wait till the fire has died down to embers, then either pour water over it (dirty washing-up water works well if you're at camp), or sprinkle sand or earth over the fire to stop it smoking and put it out.

Sometimes embers that are cold on the outside can stay warm underneath, so when the fire is cold, scrape the embers with a stick until they have all crumbled into ash. Be careful, they can be extremely hot!

Making a shelter

In the famous words of Marlene Dietrich, sometimes a girl just wants to be alone. So if you can't find any peace and solitude at home, why not make your own private den in the garden? The only problem is, it's such fun that everyone will want to join you.

YOU WILL NEED
- A sheet of plastic, a bedsheet or an old blanket
- Cord, rope or twine
- 2 forked sticks at least 1 m (3 feet) in length

STEPS

1 TAKE YOUR TWO STICKS, which should be roughly the same length and with a fork at the end. Push the non-forked ends firmly into the ground, a little bit closer together than the length of your sheet, so they stand up straight.

2 TIE YOUR CORD to the top of one stick, using the fork to stop it slipping down. Pulling it taut, stretch the line across to the other stick and tie it off with a secure knot.

3 THROW THE SHEETING OVER THE LINE and pull the edges out to make a nice tent shape, open at either end. Weigh down the edges with heavy rocks to keep them in place. If you're feeling energetic, you can camouflage your shelter with some foliage for a natural look, or tie the corners of the sheeting to nearby trees or bushes to hold the sides apart.

4 AFTER THAT, IT'S UP TO YOU – you can enjoy your solitude or you can allow the chosen few to join you in your private den.

Sleeping outdoors

In the fine weather, there is nothing better than sleeping out under the stars – but you don't have to be in some exotic foreign location. With the right gear, you can enjoy a night outdoors almost anywhere.

Why not use your newly created shelter for a night out? Or those who are made of sterner stuff can even sleep out cowboy-style under the stars, with nothing but a good sleeping bag and bed-roll.

YOU WILL NEED

- A sleeping bag
- A ground sheet or bed-roll
- A torch

STEPS

1 CHOOSE YOUR CAMPSITE CAREFULLY. Avoid deep hollows or valley bottoms where the ground tends to be wet and marshy. Also avoid solitary trees, which attract lightning, or woods where branches can drop on you. And finally, don't get too close to water or you'll be troubled by insects.

2 FIND A PATCH OF GROUND that's sheltered from the wind and as flat as possible. Clear away any stones or twigs to make a smoother surface – even tiny pebbles can feel like huge rocks under your back in the middle of the night!

3 EITHER BUILD YOUR SHELTER, or simply lay your ground sheet or bed-roll on the ground. Roll out your sleeping bag on top.

4 KEEP YOUR TORCH near the top of your sleeping bag – you may need it in the night – and then lay back and marvel at the beautiful night sky.

WARNING

Always make sure someone responsible knows where you are in case of emergencies – if nothing else, they can bring out your breakfast!

Tracking

❧

What's the point of adventuring in the wild if you're not going to see any wildlife? One of the great things about exploring is the variety of animals and birds you can see along the way. Given practice, you can learn to recognise not only the tracks of wild animals but also the other hidden signs and clues that let you know that an animal has passed by.

YOU WILL NEED
- A quiet country location
- Powers of observation and concentration

STEPS

1 ONCE YOU HAVE FOUND SOME TRACKS, work out the direction the animal is walking in, and then follow the trail.

2 STAY AS QUIET AS YOU CAN – whisper if you have to communicate, and avoid stepping on twigs and dry leaves. Experienced trackers place toe then heel when walking, rather than the conventional heel-toe step we usually use.

3 DROPPINGS PROVIDE A GOOD CLUE as to the size and type of animal and what it eats. The bigger the pile . . . need I spell it out? The same applies to birds: small and mostly liquid droppings indicate a seed-eating bird with water nearby, while small bits of bone or fur in its pellets suggest a bird of prey.

4 IF IT IS A WELL-WORN TRAIL, there's a good chance the tracks will lead back to a den or possibly to a drinking spot. If you wait patiently at these locations, especially at dawn or dusk, you may see your quarry when it comes out to feed or comes down to drink.

5 A GOOD WAY TO GET EXPERIENCE at identifying tracks is to watch an animal when it is moving on sand, snow or muddy ground and then to study the footprints it leaves behind. Some tracks of common animals are printed below to give you a head start. Good luck!

DID YOU KNOW? Footprints made in snow may appear bigger than they really are due to the snow melting, refreezing and so distorting the shape and size. This is known in scientific circles as the freeze-thaw phenomenon and scientists believe this accounts for the large Yeti footprints witnessed by so many mountaineers and locals in the Himalayas.

Some tracks you might encounter

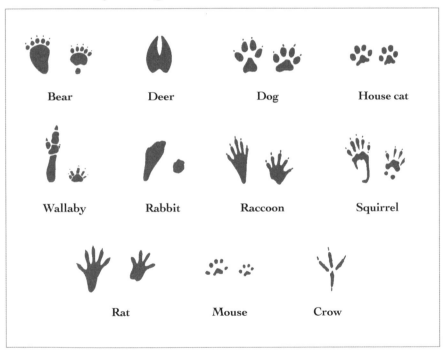

| Bear | Deer | Dog | House cat |

| Wallaby | Rabbit | Raccoon | Squirrel |

| Rat | Mouse | Crow |

Being a detective

❧❧

There have been some fantastic and famous female sleuths ranging from Miss Marple to Nancy Drew to Veronica Mars. So girls, what are you waiting for? Let's put that female intuition to the test and get on the case.

Of course, working out who did it is all a matter of the evidence – even if you have your suspicions, you need evidence to make them stand up in court. Here are some techniques that real detectives use.

Taking fingerprints

The best way to seal a case is with incontrovertible evidence and what better than the culprit's fingerprints at the scene of the crime.

> **YOU WILL NEED**
> - A pencil
> - A coin
> - A fine-hair brush (a make-up brush is ideal!)
> - Sticky tape
> - A piece of white paper or large white index card

STEPS

1 LOOK FOR OBJECTS that might have been touched by your suspect, and which might carry fingerprints. Fingerprints leave better impressions on smooth objects such as glass, metal, linoleum, varnished woods and paper.

2 USING A SOLID SURFACE, snap the lead from the end of your pencil and crunch it into tiny pieces. Use a coin on a flat surface to grind the pieces into a fine graphite powder and gently sprinke the powder over the prints in a fine layer.

3 LIGHTLY DUST THE POWDER OFF the surface with your brush to reveal the print. The powder stays attached to the oils from the suspect's skin and a fingerprint should take shape. Be sure to dust very lightly, or you may dust away the fingerprint.

4 HOLDING A SMALL PIECE OF TRANSPARENT TAPE at both ends, place the tape over the fingerprint. Press it down for a moment, then carefully pull the tape up from one end. The fingerprint will transfer onto the tape. Stick the tape on your paper or card so the black powder stands out against the white.

5 COMPARE THE PRINT with the fingerprints of your suspects. Look for marks like whorls, loops and arches, like the examples below. *Voilà!* The identity of the criminal can be revealed.

Collecting evidence

Sadly, solving crimes is not always as straightforward as finding fingerprints at the crime scene. Sometimes a good detective has to dig deeper and search for the tiniest of clues. Often you are looking for anything that will cast some light on a crime – it may be hair, fibres, handwriting, gunpowder residue, bullets, bite marks or even blood! All of these items, however gruesome, are pieces of evidence and they may be the one thing that solves the mystery.

Finding evidence and figuring out what it means is the work of a forensic science expert. Forensic experts work with police departments and lawyers to solve cases based on scientific evidence. Crime scene investigators spend a lot of time going out to find evidence on the spot. Ballistics experts concentrate on firearms and bullets, while toxicologists study harmful substances. Sometimes, forensic experts have to testify in court about what they have found.

DID YOU KNOW? Using fingerprints to identify people has been around since 1896, but now DNA 'fingerprinting' is often used to identify people based on the fact that each person has their own specific genetic code.

Code writing

Codes, ciphers and code-breaking have been around for centuries, and in wartime whole nations have sometimes depended on secret messaging systems. Nowadays, computers use sophisticated codes to keep private data – like credit-card details – safe from thieves and fraudsters.

Solving a coded message is rather like trying to translate a foreign language – you basically have to build up a 'dictionary' of the code-groups and the words that they represent. Then, given time, you can 'translate' the coded document. A cryptologist (a person who analyses and decodes codes and cryptograms) uses recognised tools to help her unravel the secrets of a text. These can range from analysing the frequency with which different symbols appear, to using computers to break down a code mathematically and find out how it works.

DID YOU KNOW? 'E' is the most commonly used letter in the English language. Cryptologists know that the symbol that occurs most often in a ciphered message probably stands for 'E'.

Deciphering a code

Put your problem-solving skills to the test with this fairly tricky cryptogram:

YMNX HTIJ NX VZNYJ INKKNHZQY. BJQQ ITSJ KTW HWFHPNSL NY

How did you get on? Takes some thinking about, doesn't it. I'm sure you've got it by now so you'll realise that each letter of the alphabet is replaced by another letter that is 5 places further down the alphabet.

Code letter: F G H I J K L M N O P Q R S T U V W X Y Z A B C D E
Deciphered letter: A B C D E F G H I J K L M N O P Q R S T U V W X Y Z

This is an example of what's known as a Caesar-shift cryptogram. Why not have a go at making up your own code and let your friends have a go at cracking it?

Solving a simple substitution cipher can be relatively easy, but you have to be a real egghead to solve even the simplest of codes. Where ciphers simply replace letters with other symbols, like the example you've just cracked, codes transform messages into completely unrecognisable forms. The inherent weakness of a code is that there always has to be a decode book for the people that use it, and finding the codebook gives you a shortcut to cracking the secrets.

Sending secret messages

Want to send a secret message that only your best friend can read? Here's how.

YOU WILL NEED
- 2 pieces of card
- Writing paper
- Paperclips
- Scissors
- A pencil or pen

STEPS

1 CLIP YOUR TWO PIECES OF CARD TOGETHER with the paperclips and, using the scissors, cut out identical windows in both sheets to make identical 'masks'. Make enough windows that you have one for each word of your message.

2 WRITE 'TOP' on the top of each sheet, and give one of them to your friend.

3 PUT YOUR MASK over a blank sheet of paper and write your message by placing a word or words in each of the windows you cut.

4 REMOVE THE MASK and write more words in the gaps to hide your message, so the page looks as though it's covered in random writing.

5 SLIP THE NOTE TO YOUR FRIEND. She can read the message instantly by putting the other mask over the top, so that the important words stand out and the camouflage words stay hidden.

Chapter Three

Beautifying

IT MAY VERY WELL BE TRUE that beauty is in the eye of the beholder, as the saying goes, but let's face it – every girl owes it to herself to make the most of what she's got. And that means giving nature a bit of a helping hand.

✦

The good news is that beautifying can be great fun, especially if you do it with your closest girlfriends. And it doesn't have to cost the earth either: rather than squandering all your hard-earned cash on salon prices, there are plenty of fun, exciting and cheap ways to create homemade beauty products that give great results.

✦

Besides, after all that outdoor adventuring, you deserve a little 'me time'. Time to get pampering, girls!

Giving a manicure

✦ ✦

Curling up in the warm to pamper your hands is a perfect way to recover after tying all those knots and braving the wind and rain. Start with a moisturising massage to relax you and protect you from dry or cracked skin, then get out the nail file and polish to shape and colour your nails.

No manicure is complete without a hand massage first, so before you start, wash and dry your hands thoroughly. Then take a concentrated hand cream and, using a small amount in the palm of the hand, rub it very quickly between the palms for about 10 seconds so that it gets warm. Hand cream is most efficient when it is absorbed with heat. Then spread it all over your hands and rub it in. Now you're ready to splash some colour on those to-die-for talons of yours!

YOU WILL NEED
- A pack of cotton wool balls
- A bottle of nail polish remover
- A nail file
- Nail clippers
- A cuticle remover
- A bottle of nail polish
- A couple of paper towels

STEPS

1 DAMPEN SOME COTTON WOOL BALLS in nail polish remover and rub your nails until all traces of old polish have been removed.

2 TAKE A NAIL FILE and rub it over the tips of your nails to remove any rough edges and to give your nails an attractive, consistent shape. If your nails have grown wildly and a nail file is not up to the job, use nail clippers first to get the rough nail shape and then tidy up and smooth with the nail file.

3 NEXT, USE YOUR CUTICLE REMOVER to gently push down the cuticle of each nail. (Your cuticle is that soft skin that forms at the bottom of your fingernail at the place where your fingernail cartilage and your skin meet.)

4 CHOOSE A NAIL POLISH from your collection – perhaps a colour that matches an outfit you plan to wear, or simply to complement your mood. Unscrew the nail polish bottle, and scrape off any excess polish that's on the brush on the inside lip of the bottleneck itself.

5 BRUSHING FROM THE BASE OF YOUR FINGERNAILS upwards towards the top tip of your nail, apply an even coat of polish to each nail.

WARNING

Remember, the colour of nail polish that you wear says a lot about you. Go for pink if you're feeling girly and sweet, and clear if 'girl-next-door' goody-goody is the look you're after. Reserve red for those occasions when you're feeling dangerous and vampish.

6 IF YOU MAKE A MISTAKE, take a paper towel and dab it with nail polish remover and try to get the excess polish off your skin using the flat edge of the paper towel. You may need to re-coat that fingernail.

7 HOLD YOUR FINGERS STRAIGHT and slightly apart immediately after applying the coat, so you don't knock or smear the polish as it dries.

8 WAIT AT LEAST 10 MINUTES before applying a second coat.

9 IF YOU APPLY SOME OLIVE OIL to your cuticles and nails before you paint them, your polish will last longer.

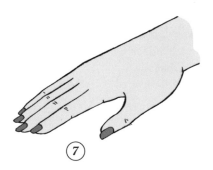

⑦

DID YOU KNOW? You can buy a quick-drying kind of nail polish at the stores, or a quick-drying sealer that sprays a clear layer over your coloured nail polish to quicken drying if you are in a hurry.

Having a pedicure

✦ ✦

When you've been trekking up and down hills – or partying the night away in your highest heels – your poor old feet tend to pay the price. So treat yourself to a relaxing home pedicure and then glam up those twinkling toes ready for another night on the town.

A foot massage is even more relaxing than a hand massage, but harder to do for yourself. Get one of your girlfriends to help you out – although you might want to wait until after you've soaked your feet clean!

YOU WILL NEED

- Nail polish remover
- Cotton wool balls/buds
- Toe nail clippers
- A large bowl
- Bath salts, bath oils or aromatherapy oils
- 125 ml (¼ pint) milk (optional)
- Cuticle remover and stick
- Foot scrub
- Pumice stone or foot file
- Foot cream
- Nail polish

STEPS

1 USE COTTON WOOL BALLS or buds dipped in nail polish remover to take off any old nail polish completely.

2 USING THE NAIL CLIPPERS, cut your nails straight across, leaving about 3 mm (⅛ inch) of length. Do not let your nail extend over the tip of your toe. For a soft square shape, file the nail around the corners, always in the same direction, using a nail file.

3 FILL A LARGE, FLAT-BOTTOM BOWL with warm water. Add a sprinkle of bath salts, or some aromatherapy oils or bath oils, and let your feet soak in the water

for several minutes. The more calloused your feet are, the longer they need to stay soaked.

4 **APPLY CUTICLE REMOVER** to your toes while they're still wet. Dab it at the base of each nail and rub it in. Wait for a minute and, using the cuticle stick, gently push the skin back where it meets the nail before dunking your feet back into the warm water.

5 **RUB YOUR FEET WITH AN EXFOLIATING FOOT SCRUB,** using a foot file or a wet pumice stone to scrub. This will remove dead skin, so concentrate on calloused areas such as the balls and heels of your feet. Remember, you're just trying to smooth the skin so don't scrub until it's red and raw.

6 **DRY YOUR FEET THOROUGHLY** with your fluffiest towel, including between the toes, and apply some nourishing foot cream to your dry feet, concentrating especially on the cuticles.

7 **APPLY A THIN COAT OF NAIL POLISH** to each nail and allow it to dry thoroughly. Polish on your toenails tends to get more wear and tear than polish on your fingernails, so it needs to be thicker – apply three or four coats in total. Take off any mistakes using a cotton wool bud dipped in nail polish remover.

8 **LET THE POLISH DRY AND HEY PRESTO** – you're ready to wear your flashiest open-toed sandals again!

9 **FOR EXTRA SOFTENING,** if your feet feel really grimy, you can add a slosh of milk to the warm water that you soak your feet in. Lactic acid in the milk helps to loosen the dead skin and makes your feet softer!

DID YOU KNOW? If nail polish is stored in the fridge it makes it easier to apply. At colder temperatures, it glides on more thickly and smoothly and in fewer coats.

Styling your hair

✦✦✦

Fashions may come and go but today you can have any hair colour or style that you like – the funkier the better. And you can dress it up with all manner of wonderful accessories – not all of which have to be bought. Did you know that the crafty trend-setting girl can design and make her own? So what are you waiting for? Let's get creative!

Plaiting your hair

Plaiting your hair is a great skill to start with, and possibly the simplest style you can wear, apart from just shoving all your hair in a ponytail. When you've learnt the basics, you can experiment with different plaits to develop your own more elaborate styles.

YOU WILL NEED
- Hair of a reasonable length
- 2 hair ties
- Hair gel or spray (optional)

STEPS

1 COMB THE HAIR, making sure there are no tangles.

2 TAKE A PORTION OF HAIR (it's easier to work with smaller sections when you're starting out) and divide into three even sections, keeping them separated with your hands and being careful not to mix them up at any stage.

3 CROSS THE RIGHT STRAND across the centre strand, so the two strands effectively switch places.

4 NOW TAKE THE LEFT STRAND and cross it over the centre strand – again so they swap places.

5 **KEEP GOING UNTIL THE PLAIT IS COMPLETE** and then secure with the elastic, scrunchie, bow or tie of your choice.

6 **IF YOU KEEP A GENTLE TENSION** on the hair as you work, that will keep the plait looking neat and tight. But don't pull too hard or you might pull hair out, which is never a good look.

7 **SPRAYING HAIR SPRAY OR GEL** on each segment of hair before plaiting can help to keep the three sections separate.

DID YOU KNOW? Combs were used at least as far back as the Iron Age, and possibly earlier. The oldest combs were made out of a slice of bone or antler, with slits carved in it to make the teeth. Just goes to show that looking good was important even before mirrors were invented!

Tying a French plait

If you've mastered a simple plait, you might want to progress to the more complicated but gorgeous French plait which is great for special occasions. But be warned, until you can do it well and quickly, your arms will really ache as you work – so it might be worth practising on a friend first!

YOU WILL NEED
- A brush or comb
- A scrunchie, tie or bobble
- Hairspray or gel (optional)

STEPS

1 **AFTER BRUSHING OR COMBING** your hair thoroughly to remove any tangles, pull a smallish section of hair back off your face. Pull it to the place where you want your plait to start.

2 **USING THE SAME TECHNIQUE** as for a standard plait, separate the section into three strands and start plaiting.

3 **AFTER A FEW CROSSOVERS,** take a small amount of hair that is hanging down on the leftside of your face and add it in to the strand on the left. Cross it over the middle strand.

4 **THEN, TAKE A SMALL AMOUNT OF HAIR** that is hanging down on the rightside of your face, and add this in to the strand on your right. Cross this over the middle strand.

5 **CONTINUE PLAITING** for a couple more crossovers and then repeat step 3 and 4.

6 **CONTINUE IN THIS WAY** until there is no more loose hair to work into the plait.

7 **YOU CAN EITHER PLAIT** the rest of the hair, or clip it at the base of the French plait and leave the bottom as a ponytail.

8 **IF YOU ARE FRENCH-PLAITING** your own hair, you can check how neat your work is by holding a hand mirror behind your head and looking at it in a bigger mirror in front of you.

WARNING

Never over-wash your hair. Excessive shampooing and use of styling aids strips the hair of its natural oils.

DID YOU KNOW? The best time to style your hair is when it is 85 per cent dry. Use a hair-dryer if you want a full, groomed look, but for natural curls and waves allow your hair to dry naturally.

Homemade hair accessories

With your hair beautifully styled, you'll need equally beautiful accessories to keep it all in place. Here are a few suggestions.

A sparkling hair clip

This gorgeous hair clip will sparkle and twinkle under the lights guaranteeing you lots of attention.

YOU WILL NEED

- A silver or gold hair clip base (or two)
- Some #4 size multicoloured bugle beads (the long ones)
- Strong white glue

STEPS

1 PUT A GENEROUS AMOUNT OF TACKY GLUE on the hair clip and, holding it by the back, carefully dip it into your saucer of beads. Use your fingers to carefully push any loose beads into the glue.

2 LET THE HAIR CLIP DRY overnight and then it's ready to wear!

A tails-down bow

When you're in a rush and you haven't got time to wash your bed-head hair, just pull it back off your face into a ponytail and secure it with this lovely bow.

YOU WILL NEED

- A 36-mm- (1½-inch-) wide ribbon (any colour or pattern you like)
- Needle and thread
- A small length of thin ribbon
- A plain bobble or clip

STEPS

1 LAY YOUR RIBBON OUT FLAT. Decide how long you'd like the tail (working from the left) and then pick up the ribbon at that point.

2 FOLD TOP LEFT LOOP OF BOW by taking the left side (tail) and looping it over the front of the right side. Hold it at junction with your thumb.

3 FOLD LOWER RIGHT LOOP by folding the length of ribbon on the right across the front of the tail at a roughly 90-degree angle. Hold in place.

4 FOLD THE LOWER LEFT BOW by continuing with the longer length of ribbon around the back of your bow, again holding it together with the previous ribbon layers at the centre.

5 THE TOP RIGHT LOOP OF THE BOW is formed by bringing the ribbon up and over from the back to the front, positioning it at a slight angle to keep it from drooping down onto the lower loop.

6 STILL HOLDING THE LAYERS TOGETHER, take your needle and thread and weave the needle through the centre of the bow (about three stitches). Your needle point should begin and end on the front of your bow.

7 WHILE THE NEEDLE IS STILL IN THE BOW, gather the centre in. Then wind the thread around the centre several times and tie it off firmly with a knot at the back of the bow.

8 NOW YOU CAN ATTACH YOUR BOW to your bobble or clip using the thin ribbon, which you then secure with a couple of neat stitches.

Spa time

✤✤

Okay, so you can't always make it to the spa, but you can bring the spa to you! With a few basic ingredients and a little pizazz, you can create the most gorgeous body-pampering products for you and your friends.

Commercial spa products can cost a fortune and are usually made out of weird ingredients that sound exotic and exciting but don't actually do your skin any good. You can save your pocket money, and have some fun, making your own spa goodies instead.

Bath bombs

YOU WILL NEED

- 225 g (8 oz) citric acid
- 450 g (16 oz) baking soda
- Witch hazel in spray bottle (only if colourant used)
- 1 teaspoon of fragrance oil
- 1 teaspoon of normal olive oil (or cocoa butter)
- Colouring of your choice (optional) – about ⅛ teaspoon of powdered colourant and ½ teaspoon of liquid colouring
- Bath bomb moulds.

STEPS

1 MIX THE CITRIC ACID and the baking soda together very thoroughly (if you don't, you get a lumpy bomb!)

2 ADD YOUR CHOSEN COLOURANT. Dry powders or speciality colourants are best but don't go mad because the colour only shows up properly once you've added the witch hazel.

3 ADD YOUR FAVOURITE FRAGRANCED OIL together with the olive oil.

4 CAREFULLY SPRAY THE MIXTURE with witch hazel, stirring all the time.

5 THE BATCH IS AT THE RIGHT CONSISTENCY when it will hold together when 'squished'. If you add too much witch hazel, it will start to fizz prematurely, so add cautiously. However, don't take too long at this stage or your mixture will go hard.

6 AS SOON AS YOU'RE HAPPY with the consistency, pack the mixture into bomb moulds, which should be left to dry for 3–4 hours.

7 ET VOILÀ! You have a selection of super-smelling, moisturising bath fizzies.

WARNING

If you add colouring to brighten up your bath bomb, it will show up any dirty 'tide-marks' in the bath by leaving a coloured ring – and your mum may not be pleased! Better get permission first, or clean the bath well after use.

DID YOU KNOW? So what makes a bath bomb froth? Any ideas? Actually, the fizzing, bubbling reaction is caused when the citric acid and sodium bicarbonate make contact with the water, releasing carbon dioxide or, to put it in non-science speak: lots of lovely bubbles.

Gorgeous soap bars

These pretty soap bars look great in your bathroom – pile them in a glass jar for maximum effect. They also make perfect gifts for friends and family.

YOU WILL NEED

- Glycerin soap, clear or white or glycerin blocks
- Soap dye in colours or your choice (available from craft shops)
- Soap or chocolate moulds
- A microwave-safe liquid measuring jug
- A spoon
- A lolly stick or coffee stirrer
- A knife

STEPS

1 IF USING BARS OF SOAP, cut into three pieces. If using purchased glycerin blocks, cut off 2–3 pre-measured chunks.

2 PUT GLYCERIN SOAP INTO A MEASURING CUP, microwave according to package directions (or 20 seconds), then in 10-second intervals until melted.

3 IF YOU WANT COLOURED SOAP BARS, now is the time to add the dye. Add a few drops and stir with a spoon. If you want pastel colours, add only a couple of drops of dye. For darker colours, simply add more dye.

4 SLOWLY POUR THE LIQUID SOAP into the mould. Set aside to harden for between 45 minutes and an hour. Rinse out the measuring cup and repeat the process for other colours if you like.

5 AFTER SOAP HAS COOLED COMPLETELY, pop them out of the moulds. If you have any difficulty, place the moulds into the freezer for 10 minutes and try again.

6 IF THE SOAPS ARE FOR GIFTS, then carefully tie a piece of ribbon or raffia around the bar for a sophisticated presentation effect.

7 FOR MULTICOLOURED LAYERS, pour the first colour in and allow it to cool until it forms a skin (about 5 minutes). Carefully and very slowly add the second colour layer over that and continue until your rainbow effect is complete.

DID YOU KNOW? The earliest evidence of manufactured soap dates back to 2800 B.C. when Babylonian clay cylinders containing a soap-like substance were excavated. However, by Roman times, the use of soap had fallen into disuse and our smelly forebears didn't start using it again until it became widely available through the mass production of the Industrial Revolution in the 1800s.

Homemade face packs

✦

When you're feeling yucky and listless and not looking your best, the first place to turn for a facial 'pick-me-up' is the larder. No kidding – fresh ingredients such as fruits and herbs nourish the skin, improve circulation and can tone and cleanse better than expensive shop-bought goodies. And they smell delicious too!

YOU WILL NEED
- Ingredients as listed below
- Liquidiser
- Somewhere to relax while the face packs work their magic

BANANA MASK

1 MASH UP A VERY RIPE BANANA. Add a couple of teaspoons of honey to make a soft, pulpy mixture.

2 APPLY TO FACE AND LEAVE FOR 10 MINUTES before rinsing off with lukewarm water, leaving a gorgeous silky finish to your skin.

STRAWBERRY MASK

1 MASH 4–6 STRAWBERRIES and apply the pulp to your face (avoiding the eyes).

2 LEAVE FOR 10 MINUTES AND RINSE OFF WITH ROSE WATER to leave your skin sparkling beautifully.

NATURAL TONER

1 LIQUIDISE HALF A CUCUMBER and strain off the juice.

2 ADD TWO TABLESPOONS OF MINT JUICE (optional), half a teaspoon of lemon juice and 2–3 drops of vinegar.

3 DAMPEN A COTTON-WOOL BALL with the liquid and use it to tone your face after cleansing.

AVOCADO MASK

1 SCOOP THE FLESH OUT of a ripe avocado and mash into a creamy pulp. Cover your face and leave for 15–20 minutes.

2 RINSE WITH WARM WATER, then spritz with toner to close the pores.

HONEY SCRUB

1 MIX ONE TABLESPOON OF HONEY with two tablespoons of finely ground almonds and half a teaspoon of lemon juice.

2 RUB GENTLY OVER FACE to exfoliate and then leave for 15–20 minutes before rinsing off with warm water.

KIWI-FRUIT WIPE

1 IF YOU'RE IN A HURRY but feel that your face needs a quick lift, simply cut a kiwi fruit in half and rub it over your face.

2 WIPE YOURSELF CLEAN WITH A SOFT WARM CLOTH and you'll look and feel better immediately.

DID YOU KNOW? Over the centuries, women have used burnt matches to darken their eyes, berries to stain their lips and young boys' urine to fade their freckles. I think we'll stick to the fruit and veg!

Skin decorations

—— ✦ ✦ ——

The art of drawing on the skin is thousands of years old – tattoos have been found on Egyptian mummies, and even Stone-Age bodies preserved in ice. Of course, the problem with tattoos is they don't wash off, and what looks cool now may be totally out of style by next year. So why not try some temporary skin adornments using henna or specialist temporary tattoo inks?

Henna tattoos

Hollywood's hottest properties are all decorating their bodies with henna (known as *mendhi*). So why not make a celebrity-style statement with your own henna adornment? The art originated in India over 5,000 years ago, and uses the crushed leaves of the henna plant to make a temporary stain on the skin in whatever pattern you desire.

YOU WILL NEED
- A henna kit (available from craft shops and the Internet)
- Eucalyptus oil
- A lemon
- A pinch of sugar

STEPS

1 WIPE THE AREA TO BE DECORATED with eucalyptus oil.

2 EITHER USE A STENCIL or create your own designs, applying the mixed henna from a piping bag onto your skin. The henna appears black when you're applying it but your finished design will look orange or dark brown.

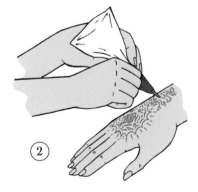

3 MIX THE JUICE OF A LEMON with a pinch of sugar to create a paste. Dab your design with the paste as this helps it to set.

4 LEAVE FOR 2 HOURS before rinsing off with warm water (some henna artists recommend that you leave it on for 4–6 hours but most of us can't sit around for that long!).

5 RUB THE AREA AGAIN with eucalyptus oil to remove any stickiness or residue.

> ## WARNING
>
> Occasionally, unscrupulous suppliers mix chemicals with henna powder and this can cause skin reactions. Test the henna on a patch of skin behind your ear and check for any reaction over the next 24 hours. Never apply henna to broken skin.

6 THE LONGER YOU LEAVE THE HENNA DYE on the skin, the darker your pattern will be and the longer it will last. On average and depending on its location, your design will fade after 2–4 weeks.

Temporary tattoos

Fancy something with a bit more colour? The beauty of these temporary tattoo kits is that you can change your image to match your mood: one day, biker babe with golden eagle; the next, a genteel lady with a discreet butterfly! What are you feeling like today?

You can get temporary tattoo kits with inks and stencils to get you started. Choose a pattern you like and some cool colours, and give it a try. Carefully wash and dry the area you want to tattoo, so it's clean and free from grease. Then press the stencil down onto your skin and daub the colour gently through it to create your pattern.

A fleecy boa

✦ ✦

Part of the beautifying process is knowing how to look stylish and fashionable while still achieving your own particular look. A boa can transform any outfit in an instant, and making your own is a great way to emphasise your own style without spending a fortune.

Making the boa

If you want to feel sumptuous after all that beautifying, you can't beat a feather boa. Think Moulin Rouge, think Marilyn Monroe, think ... not very practical for going out! You have a point. So here's a gorgeous boa that will look glamorous and still manage to keep you warm.

YOU WILL NEED

- 2 fleece cuts of different colours, each 30 cm (1 ft) wide and 150 cm (60 inches) long
- Masking tape
- A sewing machine and thread to match the colour of the fleece

STEPS

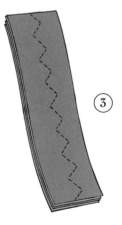

1 CUT EACH FLEECE piece in half lengthways to make four strips, each 15 cm by 150 cm (6 inches by 60 inches).

2 CUT OFF THE SELVAGES (the woven edge of the fleece fabric that stops it fraying or unravelling) so that the strips are all the same size and an even shape.

3 LAYER THE STRIPS one on top of the other, alternating the colours.

4 STITCH A NARROW ZIGZAG stitch down the centre of the strips to hold them all together. Make sure you keep them all lined up as you stitch.

5 PLACE A LENGTH OF MASKING TAPE down the centre over your stitch line. This stops you cutting your stitches in the next step and accidentally making the whole thing unravel!

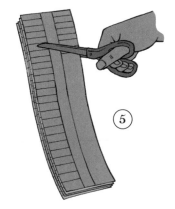

(5)

6 USING SCISSORS, CAREFULLY make cuts in from each edge, starting 2.5 cm (1 inch) from the top and working your way down at 2.5-cm (1-inch) intervals.

7 USE THE MASKING TAPE as a guide to make sure you don't cut through the stitching, and to ensure that all the fringes are the same length.

8 FLUFF OUT YOUR FRINGES and you have a fabulous and original fleecy boa that will look fantastic and keep you warm!

9 TO FURTHER ENHANCE YOUR OUTFIT, take any spare scraps of fleece that are left over and sew them to the cuffs of an old long-sleeved sweater. They'll poke out from under your jacket sleeves and look sensational, darling!

DID YOU KNOW? Feather boas have been popular since at least the 19th century, and are usually made out of ostrich or turkey feathers.

Silk-painting

The art of painting on silk originated in China, where silks were used as wall hangings, banners and even written on. Nowadays, painted silks are extremely popular all around the world.

YOU WILL NEED

- A silk scarf (long and thin in shape)
- Paper
- A pencil
- Resist or gutta serti (available from craft shops)
- Stretcher bars (also available from craft shops)
- Silk paint
- A fine brush

STEPS

1 USING PAPER AND PENCIL, draw a picture or design that you would like to paint on each end of the silk scarf.

2 TRACE YOUR DESIGN from paper to your silk scarf with a pencil by taping the drawing to a window and positioning your scarf over the design.

3 STRETCH YOUR SCARF on stretcher bars so that the fabric is taut. Trace the outlines of your design with resist or gutta. This stops the colours running together and making a shapeless mess. Make sure your line is fairly solid. If it's too thin, the dye will leak through your outline wherever it finds a weak spot.

4 IF INTRICATE DESIGNS DON'T APPEAL, you could always try painting directly onto your scarf with the colours of your choice. Use bold, thick strokes so it doesn't show too much if the colours over-run.

5 ONCE THE DESIGN IS COMPLETE, sparingly sprinkle table salt on the wet paint. Allow the scarf to dry while still flat and then brush off the salt to reveal a stunning, unique mottled design.

Customising a belt

❖

Another great clothing accessory to help beautify and revive a flagging wardrobe is the belt. Whether it's to go through trouser loops or to hang low on your hips, a little flair and imagination can transform a plain old leather belt into an eye-catchingly gorgeous accessory.

YOU WILL NEED

- An old belt (raid your wardrobe or your mum's or you can pick them up really cheaply at second-hand shops and sales)
- Craft glue
- Decorations (beads, sparkly motifs, shiny buttons – the more glittery, the better)

STEPS

1 LAY YOUR BELT FLAT.

2 PLACE YOUR CHOSEN DECORATIONS along the length of the belt.

3 WHEN YOU ARE HAPPY with your design, lift each decoration individually and glue in place.

4 ALLOW TO DRY THOROUGHLY.

5 TEAM YOUR NEW BELT with your favourite outfit and wear with style and panache.

6 IF YOUR BELT is to fit through trouser loops, make sure your decorations are not so chunky that the belt will no longer fit through.

Sewing a camisole

✤ ✤ ✤

Another good way to make yourself feel glamorous and gorgeous is to wear a luxurious camisole – after diamonds, good underwear is most definitely a girl's best friend. This easy-to-make camisole doesn't need a pattern and, when finished, will make you feel a million dollars. In fact, it's so gorgeous that it can even be worn alone under a jacket or open shirt.

YOU WILL NEED

- A length of luxurious fabric
- Scissors
- Tape measure
- A sewing machine and matching coloured thread
- Pins
- Soft mesh elastic
- Thin ribbon

STEPS

1 MEASURE FROM THE TOP OF YOUR BUST down to where you want the finished camisole to end. To this figure, add around 7.5 cm (3 inches) for a hem, and another 10 cm (4 inches) as a casing at the top. A casing is a thin tube that you will thread the elastic through.

2 WHEN YOU'VE ADDED ALL THREE measurements together, this gives you your desired width of material.

3 NOW MEASURE AROUND THE FULLEST PART of your bust. Add about 7.5 cm (3 inches), plus an allowance for the seam at the back of the camisole – about 5 cm (2 inches). Add all three measurements together and this gives you the finished length of fabric needed.

4 LAY OUT YOUR MATERIAL and cut to size.

5 FOLD THE BOTTOM of the width of material over once and over again to make a hem about an inch deep on the inside of your camisole. Pin the hem in place at intervals of about every 10 cm (4 in).

6 SEW THE HEM using the sewing machine, keeping the line as straight and neat as you possibly can.

7 ON THE OPPOSITE EDGE of the width of material from the hem, fold the edge over to make a casing through which you will thread the elastic. Again, do this on the inside of the camisole, and turn it over twice to keep it neat. Pin the casing in place as above and sew it together as you did the hem, keeping the line as straight as possible.

⑦

8 NOW SEW THE CENTRE SEAM at the back from the hem to the bottom of the casing, effectively making a simple tube top with a hem at the bottom and a casing at the top. Remember to leave an opening into the casing so that you can thread the elastic through.

⑧

9 INSERT THE SOFT MESH ELASTIC through the casing. To make it easier to thread the elastic through the casing, pin a large safety pin to the leading end of the elastic, as its rigidity makes it simpler to thread through.

10 Put the tube over your head so that the casing fits around above your bust and get a friend to tighten the elastic to a comfortable length around your chest. Once you've gathered your camisole to the desired size, take it off and sew the ends of the elastic securely together to hold them at the right length.

11 PUT ON THE CAMISOLE AGAIN. You're going to use thin ribbons for shoulder straps. Pin each ribbon at the appropriate place front and back to make the straps that will hold it securely in place. Again you may need a friend to help you with this bit.

12 REMOVE THE CAMISOLE and sew the straps onto the fabric of the top on the inside.

13 AND NOW YOU ARE READY to luxuriate in your beautiful hand-crafted camisole! Slip it on and do a twirl in front of the mirror to admire yourself and your handiwork.

⑫

14 YOU CAN PERSONALISE YOUR CAMISOLE still further by adding trim, lace or ribbon to the casing or at the hem. Just remember to attach your decoration before you insert the elastic.

DID YOU KNOW? Camisoles were originally worn over corsets or bodices: stiff undergarments, reinforced with a hard substance such as whalebone, which ladies in the 18th and 19th centuries wore around their midriff to hold their bodies in a classic 'hourglass' shape. The camisole was intended to hide the corset, to help you pretend your shape was all natural. Corsets are out of fashion now, which is a good thing since they were worn incredibly tight – so tight that you had to get a friend to lace you into one!

Sleepover parties

Having your friends round for a sleepover is blissful when it goes well but it can turn into a nightmare if you don't give it enough thought. Here are some tips to make your slumber party sublime.

YOU WILL NEED

- Your best-est, most wonderful mates
- A theme
- Your favourite DVD
- Sleeping bags/airbeds

STEPS

1 IT MAY BE SIMPLE to text or chat among yourselves when planning your party but remember to put things on a formal footing by sending proper invites. Why not have a theme? Sounds a bit corny but a spa party or crafts evening (especially just before Christmas) can be really successful.

2 NOMINATE A ROOM IN THE HOUSE where you and your friends can all sleep together, say the sitting room if your bedroom can't fit you all. Lay out your sleeping bags in plenty of time rather than waiting until everyone is tired and cranky. And don't try to change in the room where you're all sleeping – that's a recipe for lost mobiles and crushed clothing.

3 TAKE-AWAY PIZZAS are always a good staple of the sleepover but it can be fun to make your own homemade pizzas with the toppings of your choice (pre-made bases are available in supermarkets). And since you're having so much fun, it should go on record for posterity – so don't forget a disposable camera for a few candid shots.

4 AND FINALLY, THE ABSOLUTE MUST of every slumber party is your favourite film. A comedy, a romance or a weepy – doesn't matter as long as you all love it and can sit around reciting the words and re-running your favourite scenes.

Chapter Four

Feasting

IN RECENT YEARS, celebrity chefs have made cooking exciting again. The liberating feminists of last century encouraged us to hang up our rubber gloves and pinnies once, but now these culinary superstars have lured us back into the kitchen. And guess what? We're actually rediscovering that home cooking can be great fun.

◆

In this chapter, we've pulled a few recipes together that will stand you in good stead for most occasions – from rustling up a perfect picnic to baking the best pies and biscuits. And if you don't fancy all that peeling and chopping, there are some easy smoothies for a quick fruit fix.

◆

Have a go at any of the recipes that take your fancy – or try them all, and whichever one turns out best can become your signature dish!

Cupcakes

Even your most sophisticated friends will be unable to resist these divine cupcakes. They look so bright and attractive at any occasion, and they taste even better than they look.

YOU WILL NEED

- 12-bun muffin tin lined with muffin papers
- A food processor
- Oven gloves
- A wire rack
- Oven
- 125 g (4 oz) unsalted butter, softened
- 125 g (4 oz) caster sugar
- 2 large eggs
- 125 g (4 oz) self-raising flour
- ¼ teaspoon of vanilla extract
- 2–3 tablespoons of milk
- 250 g (8 oz) icing sugar
- Food colouring
- Decorations such as glacé cherries or miniature sweets

STEPS

1 PREHEAT THE OVEN to 200°C (390°F).

2 PUT ALL THE INGREDIENTS except the milk in a food processor and blitz together. When the mixture is smooth, pulse the processor while adding milk down the funnel until the mixture is a soft, fluffy consistency.

3 SHARE OUT THE MIXTURE equally between the muffin cases using a spoon. Put the cases in the oven and bake for 15–20 minutes, or until the cakes are golden on top and cooked all the way through.

WARNING

Cleanliness is very important when you are cooking, especially if you're going to share your creation. So always wash your hands, wear an apron and tie your hair back if you need to.

4 USING OVEN GLOVES, remove the cakes from the oven and place them (in their cases) on a wire rack to cool.

5 NOW FOR THE FUN PART . . . cut off the mounded tops of each cake so that you have a flat surface for icing and away you go. Top with whatever colour and whichever decorations work for you. You can make your own icing by mixing the icing sugar with a tablespoon or so of hot water and adding the food colouring of your choice.

Butterfly cakes

YOU WILL NEED

- 12 fairy cakes with no icing
- A sharp knife
- 100 g (3 ½ oz) soft, unsalted butter
- 100 g (3 ½ oz) icing sugar

STEPS

1 MAKE 12 FAIRY CAKES as before, adding a heaped teaspoon of baking powder to the flour (this ensures that your cakes will be beautifully peaked).

2 CUT OFF THE TOPS of the cakes with a sharp knife and put to one side. While the cakes are cooling, mix up your butter icing by beating the butter in a bowl and adding the sieved icing sugar gradually until it is all blended in.

3 PUT A LARGE BLOB OF ICING in the middle of each cake. Then cut the top bit of the cake in half vertically. Place both halves on top of the icing so that they resemble a butterfly's wings. What could be simpler?

The best club sandwich

The great thing about making the best club sandwich for lunch is that, although it tastes mouth-wateringly delicious, it's actually quite good for you.

YOU WILL NEED

- 2 slices of bread
- Butter or margarine
- A knife
- Cocktail sticks (toothpicks)

- Fillings (choose from ham, turkey, chicken, cheese, tomatoes, cucumber, pickles, lettuce, mayonnaise, etc.)

STEPS

1 CUT THE CRUSTS OFF the bread and spread both slices with butter or margarine. Then cut the slices in half horizontally.

2 SPREAD ONE SLICE with mustard or pickle and top with your favourite filling – ham, for example, and a slice of cheese.

3 COVER THE SECOND SLICE with mayonnaise and a layer of another filling – chicken or turkey, for example.

4 COVER THE THIRD SLICE with mayonnaise, tomato and cucumber slices, and shredded lettuce.

5 STACK THE THREE LAYERS on top of each other and top them off with the fourth slice, butter side down.

6 CAREFULLY CUT IN HALF and hold each stack together with a cocktail stick – if you've got umbrella sticks, even better!

Lemonade

Home-made lemonade is one of the nicest ways to cool down on a hot summer's day. Actually, it tastes so good, you can drink it any time of year.

YOU WILL NEED

- 250 ml (1 cup) of freshly squeezed lemon juice (about 4–6 lemons)
- 250 ml (1 cup) of hot water
- 1 litre (4 cups) of cold water
- 125–250 ml (½ to 1 cup) of sugar (according to taste)
- A small saucepan

STEPS

1 DISSOLVE THE SUGAR in the cup of hot water by heating it in the saucepan over a low heat until fully dissolved (this mixture is known as sugar syrup).

2 ADD THE LEMON JUICE and the sugar syrup to a jug.

3 ADD THE COLD WATER, until it reaches the desired strength.

4 PUT IN THE REFRIGERATOR for 30 to 40 minutes.

5 SERVE WITH ICE and a slice of lemon. Perfect!

DID YOU KNOW? An 11-year-old American boy called Frank Epperson accidentally left a glass of lemonade with a spoon in it on a windowsill one cold night in 1905, and the ice lolly was invented!

Ice cream and ice lollies

The origins of ice cream are lost in the distant past – they may start with the Roman Emperor Nero, who had slaves bring snow to him from distant mountains to make icy desserts in the first century A.D. Today, we eat more ice cream worldwide than ever before, so if you're an ice-cream addict, here's a recipe that's not only hard to beat but that is ready in just 5 minutes. No, really – give it a try.

Homemade ice cream

YOU WILL NEED

- 2 tablespoons of sugar
- 250 ml (1 cup) of milk
- 1 teaspoon of vanilla extract
- 10 tablespoons of rock salt
- Ice cubes or crushed ice
- Sealable plastic bag big enough to hold 1 litre (2 pints)
- Large sealable plastic bag big enough to hold 5 litres (8 pints)

STEPS

1 HALF-FILL THE LARGER BAG with ice and add the rock salt. Seal the bag.

2 MIX THE SUGAR, milk and vanilla together in the smaller bag, and then seal that as well.

3 OPEN THE LARGE BAG and place the sealed smaller bag (containing your ingredients) inside, and then reseal carefully.

4 SHAKE AND JOSTLE the large bag for about 5 minutes. The ice in the large bag will freeze you ingredients into ice cream. Careful not to burst either of the bags, or you'll wind up with a sticky mess, or salt-water in your ice-cream!

5 OPEN THE BIG BAG, extract the smaller bag and, before opening, wipe the opening clean to get rid of any salt. Then serve in your favourite dish (or if you're a complete ice cream freak, eat straight from the bag!)

DID YOU KNOW? On average, it takes about 50 licks to polish off a single scoop ice cream cone (though I guess that depends somewhat on the size of your tongue!)

To make ice lollies

On a sunny day, you can't beat sitting on the back step soaking up the rays and keeping cool with an ice lolly from the freezer. And the best of it is that if you invest in a set of moulds, you can invent some amazing and wacky flavours of your own. Here are a few suggestions to get you started:

Pour apple, orange, mango or any other fruit juice straight into the moulds and freeze.

Got any stewed fruit left over from another recipe? Freeze it in a mould for a great variation.

Blend your favourite fruit (strawberries work well) with yoghurt and a dash of fruit juice, and freeze in moulds for a delicious 'milk' popsicle.

Make up some jelly and pour into moulds and freeze.

Blend some watermelon (with the seeds removed) with orange juice and water and freeze the mixture.

If you don't have ice lolly moulds, don't be downhearted: you can always stick a toothpick into the centre of strawberries, raspberries or chunks of banana for an ice lolly with a difference! Why not be completely decadent and dip your fruit in melted chocolate before freezing on a tray? (You can store them in bags once they've frozen if space is an issue — not that these scrummy fruit popsicles will last that long!) For mini ice lollies, pour your chosen liquid into ice cube trays. Partially freeze, and then place toothpicks in the centre of each cube and then freeze fully.

Baking a pie

Baking a pie may sound a bit too much like something your mum used to do when she was a girl, but when you taste a slice of this heavenly peach pie, you'll realise that sometimes a bit of retro action in the kitchen may be just what's needed – your family will certainly thank you for it.

Peach pie

YOU WILL NEED
- Ready-to-roll shortcrust pastry
- 4–5 large peaches
- Water
- 110 g (½ cup) of sugar
- A saucepan
- Cornstarch
- A ceramic, glass pyrex or metal pie dish
- A rolling pin
- A fork
- Oven gloves

STEPS

1 ROLL OUT THE PASTRY and fit it over your pie plate, trimming off any excess.

2 PRICK THE PASTRY ALL OVER before baking it in an oven at 190° C (375°F) until golden.

3 MEANWHILE, BLANCH THE PEACHES by putting them in a jug of boiling water for about 20 seconds, then emptying them out and pouring cold water over them. This loosens the skin so that they are easy to peel.

4 CUT THE PEACHES INTO SLICES and discard the stones.

5 PLACE ALL BUT ONE OF THE SLICED PEACHES in a saucepan together with a cup of water. Keep one peach in reserve for later!

6 HEAT ON A MEDIUM HEAT, mashing occasionally with a potato masher or fork. Add ½ cup sugar, turn down heat and simmer for about 10 minutes.

7 IN A CUP, mix 3 tablespoons of cornstarch with 160 ml (⅔ cup) of cold water.

8 BRING THE FRUIT MIXTURE BACK TO THE BOIL and slowly stir in the cornstarch-and-water mixture.

9 COOK UNTIL THE MIXTURE IS CLEAR and thickened.

10 TAKE OFF THE HEAT and allow to cool slightly.

11 DECORATE THE BASE OF THE PIE CRUST with the last peach, which you've peeled and sliced but not cooked.

⑪

12 POUR THE COOLED FRUIT MIXTURE over the top and refrigerate. The pie-to-die-for is ready to serve whenever you and your guests (you mean you're going to share?!) want to eat.

DID YOU KNOW? Partially cooking pastry for a pie or flan without any filling is known as 'blind' baking.

Fudge

Whether you take it with you as an energy boost when hiking, or put it in a gift box and take it round to friends, fudge is the perfect little sweet treat.

YOU WILL NEED

- 750 g (3 cups) chocolate chips
- 250 ml (1 cup) condensed milk
- 1 teaspoon of vanilla extract
- A microwave or cooker
- A bowl or measuring cup (must be safe to put in the microwave)
- A square tin between 17 and 23 cm (7 and 9 inches) across
- Aluminium/tin foil to line the tin
- A metal spoon
- A spatula

STEPS

1 LINE YOUR PAN with the aluminium foil and put to one side. Pour the chocolate chips into your microwave-friendly bowl and add the condensed milk and vanilla extract.

2 PUT THE BOWL IN THE MICROWAVE and heat for 1–3 minutes. Stir the mixture and pour it into the foil-lined pan. Use the spatula to spread it around and smooth it down.

3 PUT THE FUDGE IN THE REFRIGERATOR. After 15–20 minutes, it should be ready for cutting – aim for approximately 2.5 cm- (1 inch-) square pieces.

4 LET IT COOL FURTHER, then put in a sealed plastic container and store in the fridge.

WARNING

The mixture is very, very hot when poured into the pan, and could seriously hurt or burn somebody. Take extra care.

Perfect pancakes

᛭

In France they're called *crêpes*, in America they're eaten for breakfast and in Britain they're consumed in large quantities with sugar and lemon on one specific day of the year. What are we talking about? Pancakes of course!

YOU WILL NEED

- 1 egg
- 280 ml (½ pint) of milk
- 4 heaped dessertspoons of plain flour
- Pinch of salt
- Small amount of light oil such as vegetable or sunflower oil
- A heavy-based frying pan
- Fillings of your choice

STEPS

1 IN A JUG, WHISK THE EGG into the milk. Put the flour and salt in a bowl and gradually add the milk and egg mixture, stirring vigorously all the time to remove lumps. The finished batter should be runny and have the consistency of single cream.

2 ADD A DROP OF OIL TO THE PAN and heat until hot on high heat. Add two large spoonfuls of batter and tilt the pan until it is thinly but evenly coated.

3 THE FIRST SIDE only takes about 1 minute to cook. When it's done, flip the pancake. Cook the other side and then tip onto a plate, add the filling of your choice, roll and scoff!

4 IF YOU'RE FEELING CONFIDENT, you can toss the pancake rather than just flipping it with a spatula. Shake the pan to make sure the cooked side isn't sticking to it, then swing the pan forward with a flick of the wrist. The pancake should jump out of the pan, neatly turn over, and land cooked-side-up. You might want to practise that a few times!

Planning a picnic

Whether you're attending an outdoor concert, having a day at the beach or lake, or simply heading to your local park or into your own back garden, eating *al fresco* (outdoors) is always a huge treat. So, forget the ants and wasps, pack a ball, a Frisbee or a good book, and load up your picnic hamper.

Here are a few things to think about to make sure your day goes with a swing:

Scale: Is this picnic going to be a simple snack on the run or a fresh-air feast? Are you aiming for simplicity or to impress with gourmet dining?

Guests: Who is going to be at the picnic? If it's just you and your friends, why not suggest that each friend brings a favourite dish to share.

Weather: I know, I know – you can't change the weather, but you can take a few precautions. If it's hot, make sure your food is suitably chilled, and remember the sun screen. If it's cloudy, a large umbrella can save the day.

Nutrition: Picnic food should be fun but you're still aiming for a balanced meal, so make sure you pack some healthy foods as well as treats. And don't forget something to drink!

Comfort: No-one wants to spend time sitting on wet grass or a hard rock. Pack a picnic rug or some lightweight camping chairs and you won't regret it.

Finger foods: Try and choose foods that you can eat without cutlery – wraps, crisps, etc. – to save on the washing up when you get home.

Entertainment: Depending on your location, why not pack a ball, fishing rod or frisbee? Or take some cord to rig up a makeshift volleyball net or limbo?

Be creative: Why not be adventurous and take a barbecue or plan a campfire picnic? How about a theme picnic where both the outfits and the food have to fit the theme?

Food ideas

Well that's enough to get you thinking about what sort of picnic you'd like to plan. Now, let's get down to basics and start thinking about the sort of food you'd like to enjoy on the day.

You could substitute the simple sandwich with:

Pasta, potato or rice salad in a
    sealed tub
Tortilla wraps with a favourite
    filling
Wholemeal crackers

Pizza slices
Mini pittas
Bagels
Sausage rolls
Dips

You can get your vegetable quota by adding salad items to a sandwich or wrap, or pack them separately in little pots. Try:

Cherry tomatoes
Cucumber chunks

Carrot and celery sticks
Sticks of red or green pepper

Fruit doesn't have to be boring. Why not include:

Grapes, strawberries, cherries or
    any favourite fruit in a pot.
Kiwi fruit (don't forget the spoon!)

Dried apricots, mixed fruits,
    raisins or pineapple
Ring-pull cans of fruit in juice

Every picnic needs a sweet treat. Your own home-made biscuits (see pages 108–109) would be fabulous, but any cakes, biscuits or pastries are fine.

Super smoothies

When you want a meal in a glass, the best solution is a super smooth smoothie. Packed full of nutritious ingredients – ok, and a few naughty ones too – there's really no end to the combinations of fruit you can add to make a delicious concoction that can perk you up and yet still satisfy your sweet tooth.

The nice thing about smoothies is the 'recipes' are all very simple – just combine the ingredients in a blender and blitz them until smooth.

Banana, strawberry and orange

Let's start with a classic for smoothie novices.

    1 banana
    1 handful of strawberries
    1 serving of vanilla yoghurt – about 150 ml (5 fl oz)
    75 ml (2.5 fl oz) milk
    75 ml(2.5 fl oz) orange juice
    A handful of ice cubes

Carrot smoothie

It may sound odd but this is absolutely delicious. But don't take my word for it – whiz up this quick but oh-so-healthy vegetable smoothie and see for yourself.

    500 ml (17 fl oz) of carrot juice
    125 ml (4 fl oz) of apple juice
    150 ml (5 fl oz) of vanilla or plain yoghurt
    1 banana
    3–4 ice cubes

Rise and shine

The ideal get-up-and-go meal in a glass for the girl who can't face breakfast.

175 ml (6 fl oz) of orange juice
175 ml (6 fl oz) of natural yoghurt
½ of a medium papaya (peeled, seeds removed)
1 teaspoon of lime juice (lemon juice is an alternative)
½ banana
3–4 ice cubes

Hawaiian smoothie

And now for something really exotic.

250 ml (8 fl oz) cubed peeled pineapple
250 ml (8 fl oz) cubed peeled papaya
125 ml (4 fl oz) pineapple juice or papaya nectar
1 ripe banana, peeled and cut into chunks
125 ml (4 fl oz) of vanilla or plain yoghurt
1 tablespoon of coconut milk

Smoothie top tips:

Add the liquid to the blender first and then one of the ingredients at a time, blitzing briefly (sometimes called pulsing) in between each new addition to save clogging up the blender blades.

For thick and luscious smoothies, freeze your fruit juices (the ice cube tray is ideal) and even cubes of fruit in the freezer first.

A smoothie is best drunk immediately. If left for more than 20 minutes, it may begin to separate. In this case, simply stir vigorously or put back in the blender for a quick blitz.

DID YOU KNOW? Nutritionists recommend that we eat at least 5 portions of fruit and vegetables a day. What better way to catch up on your 5-a-day than to drink a smoothie?

Iced biscuits

❖ ❖

These might look like kids' biscuits, but they have such a melt-in-the-mouth taste and buttery texture that you can serve them to anyone aged from nine to ninety-nine. Ideal for birthday parties, they're also fun and easy to make.

YOU WILL NEED

- 100 g (3 ½ oz) unsalted butter
- 100 g (3 ½ oz) caster sugar
- 1 large egg
- 275 g (10 oz) plain flour
- 1 teaspoon baking powder
- A pinch of salt
- 2 drops of vanilla essence

- Biscuit cutters
- 2 baking sheets, greased
- A food processor
- A rolling pin
- 400 g (14 oz) of icing sugar
- Water
- Food colouring

STEPS

1 BEAT THE BUTTER with a food processor until soft. Add the sugar and continue to beat until the mixture is light and fluffy.

2 BEAT THE EGG IN A CUP with a fork. Gradually add it to the butter and sugar mixture, beating all the time.

3 ADD THE FLOUR, baking powder, salt and vanilla essence to the mixture and, using your clean hands, pull the mixture into a ball.

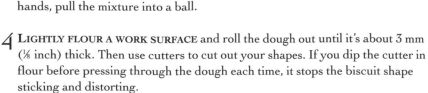

4 LIGHTLY FLOUR A WORK SURFACE and roll the dough out until it's about 3 mm (⅛ inch) thick. Then use cutters to cut out your shapes. If you dip the cutter in flour before pressing through the dough each time, it stops the biscuit shape sticking and distorting.

5 USING A FISH SLICE OR SPATULA, carefully lift the cut-out cookies onto your baking sheet.

6 IN A PRE-HEATED OVEN AT 190°C (375°F), bake the biscuits for 8–10 minutes until they are golden brown.

7 REMOVE THE BAKING SHEET using oven gloves.

8 LEAVE TO HARDEN for a few minutes and then carefully transfer them onto a wire rack to cool.

9 FOR THE ICING, first sift the icing sugar into a large bowl.

10 POUR HOT WATER FROM THE KETTLE into another bowl and gradually add spoonful by spoonful to the icing sugar, mixing thoroughly until it has a soft, firm consistency. You'll usually only need about 2–3 tablespoons of water for this amount of icing.

11 SPOON OUT THE AMOUNT OF ICING you need and add ½ teaspoon of your chosen colouring to it. Spread the icing on the biscuits with a table knife.

12 FINALLY, ADD ANY OTHER DECORATIONS: sugar flowers, small sweets, hundreds and thousands or glace cherries.

DID YOU KNOW? If you make a hole in the top of the cookies before baking, you can hang them up using pretty ribbons. This is particularly effective at Christmas if you hang your cookies on the tree – but make sure they're out of reach of the family dog!

Chapter Five

Performing

As SHAKESPEARE PUT IT, 'All the world's a stage,' and every
curious girl has her part to play. Whatever your particular
talent, there's an audience out there who would love to see
you perform, whether it's a cartwheel on the grass, a ballet
pirouette in the sitting room, a karate kick in the gym,
a spin on the ice or a song on stage. The world's your oyster
and we've got tips on how to perform all these fabulous
acts in this chapter.

✦

And for those of you who prefer to present something a little
less physical, there's advice on telling ghost stories, putting
on plays, making a speech and lots, lots more.

✦

So, to quote another great line – this time from Irving Berlin:
'There's no business like show business!' Let's get started.

Putting on a play

✦✦✦

If you've had stars in your eyes since the very first time you appeared as an angel in the school nativity play, then join us as we slap on the greasepaint and take to the boards. With a few good friends, a little rehearsal and a lot of fun, stage fright will be a thing of the past.

YOU WILL NEED
- A company of good friends or fellow thespians
- A director
- A play
- Lots of time
- An audience

STEPS

1 FIRST CHOOSE THE PLAY. Are you drawn to the Classics, or a Shakespearean tragedy? Or do you prefer the idea of a modern drama such as an Arthur Miller play? Perhaps a modern comedy is more your thing. Or you could write your own (see page 37).

2 GET THE CAST TO READ THROUGH THE SCRIPT and to tell you whom they'd like to play. If two or more people want to play the same part, then you will have to have auditions. Get all members of the cast to have a blind vote on who is best in the role.

3 IT'S TIME TO START REHEARSING THE PLAY. Firstly, you should all sit around comfortably in a room and just read the script through in character. After a few read-throughs, you need to get on stage (or in your performance room) and start rehearsing with actions and real feeling. This gives you a great opportunity to refine techniques such as voice projection (how loud or soft you speak), use of props, positions, movements and gestures, remembering your lines, exits and entrances, and general acting style.

4 A DRESS REHEARSAL, which is when you go through the play without an audience but in full costumes, is your final chance to make sure everything fits and that your play is perfect.

5 SCENERY CAN BE A PROBLEM for amateur dramatic groups. Do you know a friend or even a kind parent who has creative flair? They may agree to paint some back-drops to make your play more convincing. If not, try to keep the performance area as uncluttered and neutral as possible.

6 AND NOW, THE BIG MOMENT IS HERE. The audience is in their seats, the curtain rises and the lights dim. Daaahling, you were fabulous.

DID YOU KNOW? In theatres, actors tell each other to 'break a leg' before going on stage as a way of wishing each other luck. To wish an actor 'good luck' is actually considered 'bad luck'.

Costumes

When putting on your own play, the greatest fun can be had designing costumes. Of course, you can hire outfits from fancy dress shops, but where's the fun in that? With a little imagination and lots of pins, sticky tape and sewing thread, you can create some great costumes. Your choice of play will dictate what you create but you can always raid your parents' wardrobe or the charity shop for clothes to modify. And if all else fails, choose Shakespeare's *Julius Caesar*, which only requires an old white sheet to make a toga!

Stage make-up

If you're performing in a play, or just want to add some spice to a Hallowe'en costume or ghost story, knowing how to apply stage make-up is a great skill to have.

Make-up for your play

Stage make-up is normally thick and dramatic, and all actors – men and women! – wear it so that the audience can see their expressions even at the very back of the theatre. The make-up also helps to stop the actors' faces looking pale under the bright stage lighting.

Professional actors used to use a solid slab called greasepaint as the basis of their make-up, but as the name suggests the stuff is very greasy and unpleasant to wear, not to mention difficult to take off! Nowdays, actors use water-based make-up, which is easier to remove and less uncomfortable.

For amateur purposes, in a small room and without stage lighting, standard day make-up will be fine for your performance. Start with a light layer of foundation, to give you a nice even skin tone. Make sure your eyes stand out by applying eye-liner, and use mascara to keep your lashes good and visible. Accentuate your eyebrows with a little more eye-liner, but don't go over the top. Finally, add a little blusher and lipstick. You might scare yourself looking in the mirror – and you certainly wouldn't want to go to a party like that! – but on stage it'll look surprisingly natural.

You can also use make-up for special effects, or to enhance someone's character on stage. To make someone look older, for example, lightly draw wrinkles at the corners of their eyes and mouth, and use a dusting of talcum powder to make their hair look grey. To make someone look thin and gaunt, add dark shadows under their eyes and in the hollows under their cheekbones. And for those dramatic moments, you can easily get hold of fake blood from toy shops – just make sure it doesn't get anywhere it might stain!

DID YOU KNOW? The Ancient Egyptians and Romans used make-up containing mercury and lead – both very toxic metals.

Witch make-up

Sometimes subtle and understated just doesn't do the trick, and nothing but old-fashioned, over-the-top face-painting will do. I know, I know, you grew out of face-painting years ago. But no girl is too old for this fabulous witch look, which can be great for spooky performances at Hallowe'en parties, or any time you want to dress up. With a few deft paint strokes, plus a black hat and cloak, you'll be a winner on any spooky occasion.

YOU WILL NEED

- Face paints or stage make-up in green, black, sparkly silver or gold and sparkly white
- A make-up sponge
- A make-up brush

STEPS

1 USING A SPONGE, apply a fine layer of sparkly white face paint all over your face as a base for your design.

2 AGAIN WITH A SPONGE, apply a covering of bright green around your forehead, the sides of your face, and your chin and nose. Blend it in with the base layer for a greenish-white tinge, rather than aiming for a complete covering.

3 USING A MEDIUM BRUSH and black face paint, paint on some flamboyant wavy eyebrows. Fill in your lips with black and draw a thick line under your eyes, sweeping from the middle of each eye out toward the temples – very vampish.

4 ADD A SPOOKY COBWEB on one cheek in black paint, complete with spider.

5 FINALLY, OUTLINE SOME OF THE SPIDER WEB with sparkly gold or silver face paint for a finishing touch.

Telling a ghost story

If you don't like scary movies, you should probably turn the page now. But for those of you who are made of sterner stuff, here's a way to scare your friends witless with a spooky ghost story.

YOU WILL NEED

- A torch
- Candles and matches
- An accomplice

- A fan
- A CD player and recordings of spooky music and/or sound effects

STEPS

1 CHOOSE A SCARY GHOST STORY from a book and memorise it. Secretly recruit a friend to help by providing some 'special effects'.

2 SET THE SCENE by playing scary background music – you know the kind of thing: creepy organ music in a minor key.

3 CAREFULLY LIGHT SOME CANDLES OR TEA-LIGHTS around where you'll be sitting, and turn out all the other lights. If you are outdoors, light a campfire (see page 55) and set up some flickering candles.

4 INVITE YOUR AUDIENCE in and take your place centre-stage. Shine a torch under your chin for extra spookiness.

5 HEIGHTEN THE TENSION by speaking in a soft voice so people have to concentrate if they want to hear. At a crucial moment, your accomplice should slip away from the group and use a fan to make the candles flicker, or bang a door to send a shiver of fear down your listeners' spines.

6 WHEN YOU GET TO THE FINAL PART, raise your voice for dramatic effect. Get your accomplice to scream at the scariest moment – or scream yourself, if you're feeling brave.

Juggling

✦✦✦

These days you don't have to join the circus to learn juggling. Here's how to juggle three balls – a trick that's bound to impress your friends.

YOU WILL NEED
- 3 soft juggling balls or small bean bags

STEPS

1 START BY HOLDING TWO BALLS in your right hand and one in your left. Throw one of the balls in an arc from your right hand and catch it with your left. Now, simply throw the ball back again.

2 THE NEXT STEP STARTS OUT THE SAME. Throw one ball from your right hand in an arc to the left hand. As the ball reaches the top of its arc, throw the ball in your left hand over to your right. Catch the first ball in your left hand, and the second ball in your right.

3 NOW FOR THE FULL CASCADE. Throw one ball from your right hand up and to the left. Almost immediately, throw the ball in your left hand up and to the right, just as you did above.

4 AS YOU CATCH THE FIRST BALL in your left hand throw the third ball from your right hand into the air, just before you catch the second ball in that hand. Then catch the third ball in your left hand.

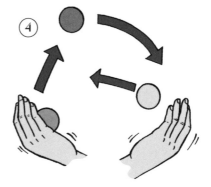

Being a popstar

✦✦✦

Whether you love to hog the microphone or prefer to limit your performances to singing in the bath, music is a feature of all our lives. If you find yourself humming along to the radio in the car and dream of taking part in a TV talent show, then it's time to polish up your raw talent. So let's get this musical extravaganza on the road.

Singing like a pop idol

YOU WILL NEED
- A song to sing
- Somewhere private to practise

STEPS

1 CHOOSE YOUR SONG CAREFULLY. Do you fancy a bluesy little number or are you in the mood for pure pop? Pick a song you love to listen to. A word of caution though – unless you have a great voice, avoid songs by divas like Whitney Houston and Mariah Carey – it's just too much of a vocal challenge.

2 FIND THE LYRICS to your chosen song and learn them. There's nothing worse than a performer who has to break into 'la la la' halfway through.

3 GET THE LOOK RIGHT. Whether it's a karaoke evening or a concert, it helps if you look the part. Be as glitzy, glam and showbiz as you like.

4 PERFORMANCE AND SHOWMANSHIP are a large part of a singer's success, irrespective of vocal talent – so if you don't have the voice of an angel, make sure you make up for it by giving a larger-than-life performance. Only those with great voices can get away with standing in front of the mike and just delivering a song.

Writing song lyrics

Perhaps you'd prefer to leave the singing to those who crave the spotlight. If you're more of a backroom girl, why not write the lyrics to a song?

Why not pick a subject dear to your heart and set your thoughts to paper? It's like writing poetry, but a song has verses and a chorus to connect the verses together. It's not essential for the lines of the verse to rhyme, but an audience tends to expect it somehow.

Once you've read and re-read your lyrics and made any changes, you might like to think about composing the music to accompany your words. If that's not your bag, then perhaps you have a friend who is musically inclined who might like to collaborate with you. No? Well how about choosing a favourite song and writing your own lyrics to fit the music – that's a good place to start.

Playing guitar

Many of the most famous songs use only three or four different chords. You can find the chord patterns in song books or on the Internet, and practise away until the song comes together. Learn the position of the fingers on the strings for each chord and then rehearse playing them in the right order. Get it right and who knows, you could find yourself on stage!

One important step is to hold your instrument properly. Sit down with the chair at a height that keeps your thighs parallel to the ground. Rest the dip in the side of the guitar on your leg, on the same side as your strumming hand. Angle the face of the guitar slighty towards you and try not to hunch your back.

DID YOU KNOW? In the 1960s, legendary rock guitarist Jimi Hendrix revolutionised guitar playing. He amazed audiences by coaxing never-before-heard sounds from his guitar, which he played upside down, behind his back and even with his teeth!

Ice skating

✣✣✣

The experts make it look so simple, don't they? In fact, ice skating is actually quite hard to learn. Confidence on the ice is essential before you can start to perform, but once you've got the hang of gliding around the rink, you can move on to more advanced moves such as a spin!

YOU WILL NEED
- An ice rink
- A pair of ice skates
- Warm clothing and gloves

SCULLING

1 IF YOU POSITION YOURSELF CORRECTLY to start, the rest will follow. So move about an arm's length from the barrier and stand with your feet about hip distance apart and both of your blades facing in the same direction. (Don't worry – you can grab the barrier if you need to from here.) Keep your arms out, away from your sides, for balance.

2 RELAX YOUR ANKLES and let your feet turn into a slightly pigeon-toed position, toes pointing inwards. Bend your knees (look down if it helps at the beginning, but don't get into the habit of looking at your feet – it's not good once you can skate).

3 AS YOU ALLOW YOUR FEET TO DRIFT TOGETHER, you will glide forward. When they are a few inches apart, point your toes out and your feet will drift apart. As they reach hip width again, bend your knees a little more and go back to the pigeon-toed position.

4 AS YOU GO IN AND OUT of the pigeon-toed position, you will drift gently forwards, leaving a scalloped pattern on the ice. The more you bend your knees, the faster your forward swizzles will become.

SPINNING

1 SPINNING IS THE BEST PART of figure skating for girls – it looks fantastic and so elegant, but don't attempt this until you're confident at gliding around the rink. The first spin to learn is the two-foot spin, where you keep both blades in contact with the ice. You can spin either to the right or to the left, whichever feels most natural for you.

WARNING

It is almost impossible to judge the thickness of the ice on frozen lakes and ponds, so you should never go skating outdoors on the ice without permission or someone in attendance.

2 START WITH YOUR FEET about hip distance apart. Stand with your back straight and your chin raised and your arms curved at chest height in front of you to form a loose circle. Now place the right toepick (front tip of the blade) into the ice.

3 NEXT, BRING YOUR LEFT ARM around in front of you and your right arm back behind you, with the palms facing down. Let your left foot follow around as you move your arms.

4 AS YOU BRING YOUR ARMS briskly back to the front, rounded circle position, keeping your feet still at hip width apart, you should start to turn. Allow yourself to turn through a whole revolution.

5 IF YOU REMEMBER TO KEEP LOOKING UP, you may even get two turns or more from this move (looking down slows the spin and makes you feel dizzy!)

6 KEEP PRACTISING and if you find that you're moving across the ice rather than staying in one spot, then try turning your right foot in slightly as this can help to keep the spin centred. If you want to look and feel like a real figure skater, then you must make sure your posture is good: shoulders down, back straight and chin up. Ta da – a real star in the making! Got that nailed? Probably time to start looking at sparkly ice-dresses then.

Ballet

✦✦✦

Not all little girls want to wear pink leotards and attend ballet classes. But this classic dance form is the basis for many modern styles such as jazz dance, and it can be helpful to have a few basic ballet moves tucked under your tutu.

The pirouette

The pirouette has to be the classic ballerina movement. Here's how to pull one off like a professional.

YOU WILL NEED
- A leotard or loose-fitting dance clothes
- Ballet shoes or soft-soled dance shoes

STEPS

1 START WITH YOUR LEGS TIGHT TOGETHER and feet turned outwards, with the heels overlapping. Your arms are held in front of the body slightly curved so that the tips of the fingers almost meet, resting on the thighs.

2 MOVE YOUR BACK LEG OUT TO THE SIDE, with the toes pointed, and your arms moving to your sides, a little below shoulder height and slightly curved.

3 RETURN YOUR LEG TO THE STARTING POSITION but raised in front of the supporting leg with the knee bent. At the same time, hold your arms in front of you at chest height with fingers almost touching.

4 USE THE MOMENTUM FROM THE LEG MOVEMENT in step 3 to begin your turn. Keep your eyes facing forwards for as long as possible by looking over your shoulder, then snap your head round to look forward again as you spin.

The arabesque

The arabesque may look easy, but it's one of the most demanding exercises for a ballerina to perform.

YOU WILL NEED

- Clothes and shoes as before
- A bar or tall-backed chair

STEPS

1 START BY STANDING WITH YOUR HEELS TOUCHING, and your toes pointed apart at about 45 degrees. Your arms should be held as they were when you started the pirouette: in front of the body and slightly curved.

2 MOVE YOUR RIGHT LEG FORWARDS, toe first, so it's about half a pace in front of you. Stretch your right arm out forwards, holding your hand about level with your shoulder.

3 SLOWLY LEAN FORWARDS and shift your body-weight onto the ball of your right foot. As you do so, lift your left leg straight up behind you. Stretch up with your right arm, and back and slightly up with your left arm.

4 RAISE YOUR LEFT LEG AS HIGH AS YOU CAN – try to get your foot level with your hips, and your toe pointed at the ceiling. (You might need to practise a while to get flexible enough to do this – be careful not to overstrain yourself the first few times!)

5 TO FINISH, BRING YOUR BACK LEG down in a controlled movement, and put your left foot on the floor in front of your right, so your legs cross. Bring your arms back to their starting position as you lower your leg.

Synchronised swimming

✦✦✦

If you want to have some fun with a group of friends and stay fit, have a go at synchronised swimming. This sport demands good water skills combined with strength, flexibility, agility, good timing and grace – oh, and the ability to hold your breath. And it's almost exclusively performed by women – perfect!

Before you can start devising routines, you have to master a couple of the basic strokes. Once you've got the hang of these, you can string together a few moves and choreograph them to your favourite tune. If you have long hair, make sure it's securely fastened in a ponytail before you start, or you won't be able to see your friends in the water for swirling hair!

YOU WILL NEED

- A swimming pool
- A swimming costume
- Friends who can swim

⚠

THE SUPPORT SCULL

1 THIS KEEPS A SWIMMER STABLE and in position when she's performing upside-down underwater. Get into position by duck-diving under the water and turning upside-down, with your legs straight up and as far out of the water as possible.

2 TO MAINTAIN THIS POSITION, keep your upper arms close to your sides, and your lower arms bent so they stick out at right-angles to your body.

3 NOW MOVE YOUR LOWER ARMS back and forth, while keeping your elbows by your sides. Balance your movements to support your upside-down position. Practise until you can stay perfectly stable upside-down. Then you can move on to some more complicated moves.

THE EGGBEATER

1 THIS LEG MOVEMENT KEEPS the swimmer stable in the water, leaving her arms and hands free. Start in a sitting position, with your back against the side of the pool and your thighs parallel to the bottom of the pool.

2 MOVE YOUR LEGS AS FAR APART AS POSSIBLE and flex your feet up, with your knees high. Kick your right leg out to the side, around in a circle, and back to its original position against the wall. Then do the same with your left leg. Your legs should pass each other in a constant eggbeater movement.

3 ONCE YOU ARE CONFIDENT, move into deeper water and practise without using the wall for support until you can float without using your arms.

All you have to do now is to learn a few standard moves, which you can then string together with your friends into a routine. Use the eggbeater to perform graceful arm movements, and sculling for some of the following leg moves:

Ballet leg: Float on your back with one leg extended vertically while the other stays straight along the surface of the water.

Vertical bent knee: Start with the support scull, but instead of having both legs vertical, bend one leg with the toe touching the inside of the vertical leg.

Splits: While upside-down, move your legs into a splits position, if you can manage it, on the surface of the water.

Crane: Again while upside-down, extend one leg straight up, keeping the other parallel to the surface of the water.

DID YOU KNOW? The sport was developed in the early 1900s in Canada. It was originally called 'ornamental swimming'. It became an Olympic sport in 1984.

Gymnastics

Being able to perform a few basic gymnastics moves is a great way to impress, and a fun way to keep fit. Here's how to perfect the handstand, the basic gymnastics move, and the slightly more challenging cartwheel – the bread and butter of all gymnasts!

YOU WILL NEED
- Plenty of space
- Soft, flat ground (if outdoors)
- Soft landing mats or carpet (if indoors)

HANDSTAND

1 STAND STRAIGHT AND lift your arms above your head, keeping them straight and close to your ears. Take a big step forward with one leg. With your upper body straight, tip forward over the front leg, pushing with your back foot.

2 AS YOUR HANDS APPROACH THE GROUND, keep your arms straight and don't let your shoulders droop. As your weight transfers to your hands, push up with your legs and straighten out completely, holding your core body muscles tight. Once you're upright, keep your body straight to prevent you toppling sideways.

3 LOWER YOUR LEGS BACK DOWN the way they came with control. You can practise against a wall until you build up strength and balance.

4 IF YOU'RE AFRAID of falling, imagine someone supporting you, or try falling a few times on purpose so that you know it won't hurt. The best way to fall from a handstand position is to bend your arms and tuck into a roll.

WARNING

Always warm up and stretch before starting any gymnastics move to prevent pulling a muscle. Remember to stretch your wrists before and after a handstand or cartwheel.

CARTWHEEL

1 STRAIGHTEN YOUR ARMS above your head, keeping them close to your ears, and reach for the sky! Point your leading foot in the direction you want to go and turn the other foot slightly out (this helps you to balance).

2 REACH TOWARDS THE GROUND with the same hand as your pointed foot, which will have to bend slightly as you lean down (so if your right foot is pointed, then it's your right hand that moves first) and follow with the other hand.

3 AS THE FIRST HAND IS GOING DOWN, the opposite foot is coming up – kick strongly so your legs come off the ground and you end up balancing your weight on your arms, rather like with the handstand, with your legs straight and out in a straddle position. Keep your back straight and your hands straight and firm – your body should be in a straight line from shoulders to hips.

4 LAND ON THE OPPOSITE FOOT from the leading foot – you should end up in the same position that you started in, but with the opposite leg forward and slightly bent. Straighten up. Well done! You've landed a perfect cartwheel.

5 ALL OF YOU – your arms, body and legs – should be in a straight line throughout this move. It may help to picture yourself as the spokes of a wheel as it goes around.

DID YOU KNOW? International gymnasts can perform wonderfully graceful flips, walkovers and turns on a beam which is only 10 cm (4 inches) wide! They start by practising handstands and cartwheels in the gym.

High jump

✦✦✦

The high jump has been an Olympic event since Ancient Greece. Here are some useful techniques to help you gain some height.

YOU WILL NEED
- A high jump bar with landing mat
- Space for a run up
- Sports clothing and trainers

⚠️

STEPS

1 SPRINT TOWARDS THE BAR in a curving approach to gain the right speed and angle. Take off on the foot furthest from the bar – so your left foot if you're approaching from the right – and push yourself upwards using your leading leg to twist your body over the bar.

2 THINK ABOUT LYING BACK with your arms at your sides, your back arched, and your hips pushed forward as you go over.

3 LIFT YOUR FEET after you've cleared the bar so you don't knock it off with your heels.

4 YOU CAN SUFFER SERIOUS INJURY attempting a jump without proper equipment, so make sure you're supervised by an experienced jumper the first few times you try.

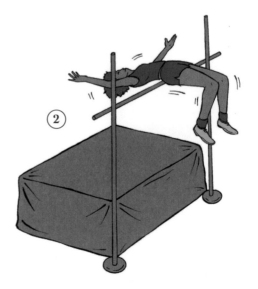

Making a speech

❖❖

You never know when you may be called upon to make a speech. It could be at school or college, or a special family occasion. Either way, every girl needs to know how to speak in public with confidence and without making a fool of herself.

YOU WILL NEED
- Pens and paper
- Some peace and quiet
- Inspiration

STEPS

1 ABOUT **90** PER CENT OF MAKING A GOOD SPEECH is the preparation. Start by thinking through what you want to say. Consider your audience and tailor your language to them – keep an informal tone for friends and family, more formal for strangers. Think also about the purpose of your speech.

2 DECIDE ON A STRUCTURE for your speech. It should have an introduction, where you explain the reason for your speech and why the audience should listen to you; a main body, where you cover the main content of your speech; and a conclusion, when you recap the main points and emphasise the bits that you want the audience to remember.

3 ONLY NOW CAN YOU START WRITING. Then re-read and edit your speech until you are happy with it. Then practise your speech so that you're word perfect (some public speakers practise in front of a full length mirror).

4 ON THE DAY, TRY TO REMAIN CALM. When it's time, take a few deep breaths, stand tall and smile – you will have your audience in the palm of your hand. Remember that the audience wants you to succeeed. Don't view them as an enemy – make them a partner and talk to them as you would a group of friends.

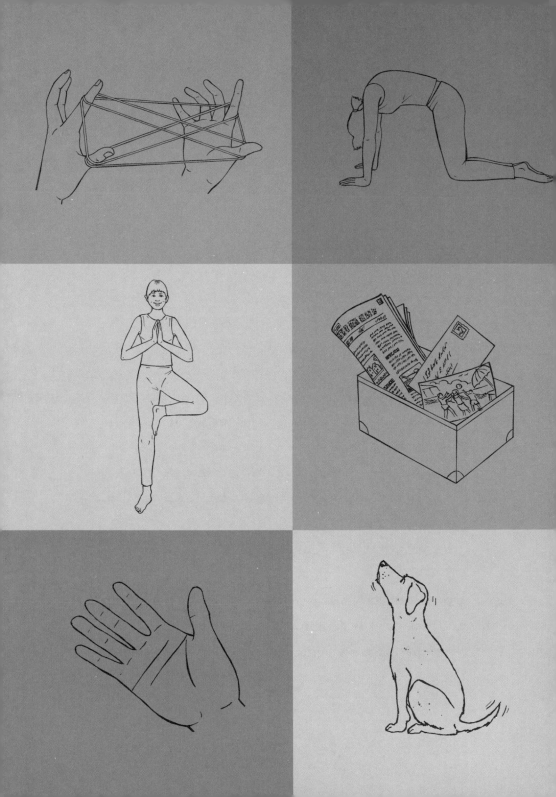

Chapter Six

Playing

AFTER ALL THE EFFORT that you've been putting in to adventuring in the previous chapters, now seems like a good time to slow down the pace a little, kick off your shoes, and chill out.

✦

That doesn't mean that the fun has to stop, though. Far from it! This chapter is packed full of exciting ideas for games, tricks and activities that range from mastering a killer smash in table tennis, to magic tricks that will amaze and delight your friends. We've even got the family pet involved, with suggestions for games to play with your dog.

✦

And if you really are feeling a little weary, why not plump up the cushions on your favourite couch and learn how to play some fantastic card games, cat's cradle or the ancient Chinese game of Mahjong?

Skipping

✦✦

Skipping is a great way to keep fit, and it's great fun! It's one of the few games you can play on your own or with your friends, and it's unisex so you can play with your brothers as well – if you're unlucky enough to have any (only joking!) Use these jumps and tricks to make up games with your friends.

YOU WILL NEED
- A skipping rope
- Bags of energy!

BASIC JUMP

1 HOLD THE HANDLES of the rope in each hand with the rope looped behind you.

2 SWING THE ROPE over your head.

3 KEEPING BOTH FEET TOGETHER, as the rope comes down in front of you towards the ground, jump over it.

4 REPEAT THIS 10 TIMES or until you get tangled up, whichever comes first.

FRONT STRADDLE

1 TURN THE ROPE AS BEFORE, but this time jump with one foot in front of the other.

2 AS THE ROPE COMES ROUND AGAIN, jump again but switch the position of your legs.

JOGGING STEP

1 AS YOU TURN THE ROPE, step over with one foot.

2 ON THE NEXT TURN of the rope, step over with the other foot.

3 AS THE NAME IMPLIES, it's just like jogging on the spot but with the rope.

DOUBLE TURN

1 START WITH A NORMAL, single bounce.

2 THEN JUMP HIGH INTO THE AIR and turn the rope fast so that it passes beneath your feet twice before you land. This is a more advanced trick, and you'll need to jump high and turn the rope as fast as you can. Good luck!

FRONT CROSS

1 DO A NORMAL JUMP with the first turn of the rope.

2 AS THE ROPE COMES AROUND for the next turn, cross your arms in front of you and jump through the loop it makes.

3 TRY ALTERNATING front-cross jumps with normal jumps for a bigger challenge.

Try to land on the balls of your feet and bend your knees on landing to absorb the shock. Keep your arms at your sides and turn the rope with your wrists, so the arm movements stay small. If you're finding a jump difficult, rehearse the moves without the rope for a few turns and then try again with the rope – you'll be surprised how much that can help.

DID YOU KNOW? Professional boxers use skipping as part of their fitness training.

Hopscotch

This traditional playground game never loses its appeal. Just watch – even the crustiest adult can't resist having a go if he or she sees a hopscotch grid chalked out in the street, particularly if they think no-one is looking!

YOU WILL NEED
- Chalk (different colours if possible)
- A hard surface to mark out your grid
- A stone for each player to use as a marker
- Some friends to play with

STEPS

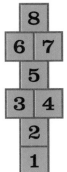

1 USING THE CHALK, draw out your grid as in the diagram. Start by throwing your stone into square one.

2 HOP YOUR WAY to the end of the grid. Hop on one leg into single squares, and jump with one foot in each square where there are two side by side.

3 WHEN YOU GET TO THE TOP, swivel round and hop all the way back down the grid, picking up your marker as you go.

4 IF YOU STEP ON A LINE while hopping, or put both feet down in the same square, it's the next player's turn and you repeat square one on your next turn. If you hop successfully, it's the next player's turn, but you get to move to square two on your next turn.

5 ON THE NEXT ROUND, throw your marker into the next square and hop again, and keep going until you've completed the grid. If your marker lands in the wrong square, you miss a go. Whoever gets to the end of the grid first wins.

Karate kicking

If your ideal role-model is tomb-raiding Lara Croft, or one of those all-action Charlie's Angels, then you'll need to add the karate kick to your repertoire if you're to take on the role of a feisty heroine.

YOU WILL NEED
- Loose clothing
- A reasonable amount of space
- A volunteer
- Lots of padding

STEPS

1 STAND WITH YOUR LEFT LEG slightly forward, knee bent over the heel of your foot, and with your weight on the forward leg.

2 BRING YOUR RIGHT KNEE UP as far as you can with the knee bent and the toes pointing to the ground.

3 NOW EXTEND THE LEG with a quick snapping action and, as you make contact with your target (a trusting friend holding a cushion, perhaps), exhale. Your aim is for the bony ridge behind your toes to make contact rather than any other part of the foot.

4 AFTER IMPACT, bring your leg back to the original position with the knee bent, ready for another kick.

- -
DID YOU KNOW? The kick described here is known as the 'snap kick' but there are many different styles you can perform in Karate.
- -

- - - - - - - - - - - - - - - - - - -
WARNING
- - - - - - - - - - - - - - - - - - -

Karate moves are designed for self-defence, and that's all they should be used for. Practising for fun is fine, but make sure your volunteer has enough padding to protect themselves, and never attack when they're not ready.

Yoga

✦ ✦

One of the greatest assets of any girl is the ability to project a calm and serene exterior, even if you're panicking inside. And one of the best ways to perfect this Zen quality is to practise yoga. So here are a few basic yoga poses to whet your appetite.

YOU WILL NEED
- Comfortable clothing that allows plenty of movement
- Some floor space

THE CAT

1 START ON YOUR HANDS AND KNEES, hands directly under your shoulders. Breathe in, then as you breathe out, slowly arch your back, rounding your spine and dropping your head. Look towards your navel.

2 BREATHING IN SLOWLY, return to the neutral position that you started in. As you breathe out, let your back sink down slowly, keeping your head where it is.

3 PUSH YOUR BOTTOM RIGHT UP and out and raise your head so you can see as much of the ceiling as possible. You may find that your elbows try to bend – don't let them. They need to be absolutely straight for maximum effect, although they shouldn't be locked.

4 AS YOU BREATHE IN, return to the neutral position.

5 REPEAT THE ENTIRE MOVEMENT two or three times and then relax. Believe it or not, this gentle exercise makes your spine more supple, firms the bottom and strengthens the shoulders and arms. Wow!

THE COBRA

1 LIE FACE DOWN with your arms at your sides and your feet together – toes straight out behind you. Place your hands flat on the floor just below your shoulders, next to your ribs. As you breathe in, gently push up with your hands, and as your head and chest lift off the ground, start to arch your back. Stop when you reach your comfortable limit. Hold for a count of five.

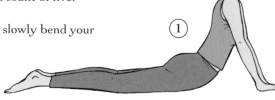

2 KEEPING YOUR HEAD BACK, slowly bend your elbows and lower yourself back down to the floor again. Finally drop your head gently to the ground.

THE TREE

1 STAND UP STRAIGHT with your arms at your sides. As you breathe in, shift your weight onto one foot. Then, breathing out, bend one knee and place the sole of that foot as high as possible on the inside of your other thigh (you can help with your hand to begin with). Keep your toes pointing down your thigh, turn your arms outwards for balance and breathe steadily.

2 NOW RAISE YOUR ARMS until they are level with your shoulders and stretch them out. Then bring the palms together in a prayer position in front of you at chest height.

3 LOOKING STRAIGHT AHEAD, take a breath and raise your arms over your head, keeping the palms together and stretching up. Keep the bent knee pushing back and your hips facing straight ahead, while lifting up from the waist.

4 RETURN YOUR ARMS TO YOUR SIDE and slowly return your foot to the ground. Keep looking straight ahead and focus with your eyes on a point in front of you to help you to balance.

Winning at table tennis

✦✦

Table tennis – also known as ping pong – is a fast and skillful game that demands good reactions. It is the third most popular sport in the world with over 300 million players worldwide. What's more, it's one of the few games where boys and girls can play on an equal footing because a player doesn't require brute strength to win – technique is more important.

If you want to be able to hold your own at ping pong, you need to have a good serve and a killer smash. Master these techniques and you'll have cracked it!

YOU WILL NEED
- A table tennis table
- 2 table tennis bats
- A few table tennis balls
- An opponent

THE SERVE

1 STAND BEHIND THE END OF THE TABLE, holding the ball in the palm of one hand and the bat in the other.

2 TOSS THE BALL UPWARDS about 15–30 cm (6–12 inches) and hit it at the top of its arc. It needs to bounce once on your half of the table (in front of the net) and then once on your opponent's half. In singles games, the ball can land anywhere on your opponent's side of the net, whereas in doubles games, it must be served diagonally from the right-hand side of your court into the left-hand side of your opponents' court, just as in lawn tennis.

3 IF YOUR SERVICE IS 'GOOD', then your opponent must return the ball before it bounces on her side of the table a second time. Having service is an advantage because it's hard to return a serve, particularly since you can vary where you place the ball and the speed at which you hit it.

4 CONVERSELY, IF YOUR SERVE HITS THE NET and does not land on your opponent's side, then they win the point. If it hits the net and goes over to bounce on her side, that's called a 'let', and you take the serve again.

5 ONCE YOU'VE MASTERED THE BASIC SERVE, you can confuse your opponent by varying your style between slow serves with lots of spin and faster serves.

THE SMASH

1 YOUR OBJECTIVE WITH A SMASH is to hit the ball so fast that your opponent simply can't return it. You have to wait during a rally for the perfect time to execute a smash shot – usually when your opponent has returned the ball and it bounces high and close to you.

2 THEN YOU SEIZE YOUR CHANCE – take a big back-swing and hit the ball with as much speed as possible onto her side of the table.

3 DON'T REST ON YOUR LAURELS JUST YET – if she does manage to return your smash, you've got to be on your toes and ready to smash the ball back again until you finally produce the winning shot.

4 THIS IS YOUR TRUMP CARD when playing table tennis. A good smash moves your opponent out of position and can force her off balance. Her return shot then has to be defensive and you can reply with more smash shots until you win the point.

DID YOU KNOW? Table tennis originated in England in the 1880s as an after-dinner amusement for upper class Victorians. World-class table tennis players can smash the ball at speeds of 112.5 kmph (70 mph)!

Playing with your dog

＊

A dog is supposedly man's best friend (while diamonds are a girl's), but that shouldn't stop an adventure-loving girl getting in on the fun and games. If your dog likes to play, here are some ideas that he'll love, and which will improve the communication and understanding between you and your favourite pet.

Find the treat

YOU WILL NEED
- A friendly hound
- Dog treats or your dog's favourite tit-bit (my dog loves little cubes of cheese)
- Plenty of patience

STEPS

1 GET YOUR DOG to sit and stay while you hide the treats in places around the room (you will probably need to keep repeating the command to stay).

2 WHEN YOU SAY 'GO' your dog can race off and collect the treats.

3 START BY HIDING ONE or two treats and slowly build up the numbers as he learns the game. If he won't stay, remove the treats.

Hide and seek

Once your dog is good at sitting and staying, the above game works just as well as a version of hide and seek. While your dog waits, you find somewhere to hide and then call the dog and see how long it takes for him to find you.

Jumping

Start with small obstacles (a sturdy book is enough of a challenge for a puppy) and encourage your dog to jump over them. Lavish him with praise if he succeeds. With practice, dogs can learn to jump quite high obstacles – but be warned, this trick can backfire spectacularly if your dog learns to jump over the garden fence!

Obstacle course

Set up an obstacle course in your garden. It might include cones to weave through, a barrier to jump over, and even a plank bridge or something similar to walk across. A children's tunnel is a fun addition to the course – you should run to the other end and call your dog through. If your dog is nervous about the plank bridge, let him get used to crossing wider bridges with two or three planks to build up his confidence.

Ball games

Many dogs love fetching and retrieving a ball or stick. Start throwing a ball when your dog is a puppy, keeping the distances quite short to begin with, and enthusiastically encourage him to bring it back to you. Make a big fuss when he does and then you will be able to extend the distance that you throw the ball.

Frisbee

Not all dogs immediately understand the concept of the game. To start, throw your frisbee straight to your dog at a short distance. Once he knows how to catch the disc, it's a small step to running to catch it. You can then start to throw the frisbee higher and higher until it goes over your dog's head. At that point, your dog will instinctively know to turn around and chase the disc.

DID YOU KNOW? Believe it or not, there are now competitions for dogs involving owners throwing and dogs catching a frisbee – imaginatively called 'frisbee dog' or 'disc dog' competitions. Mind you, that'll be no surprise when you see how much fun can be had.

Wacky races

You don't have to wait until sports day to have some fun. These races are a great way to idle away some hours with your friends, and far too much fun to be the preserve of little children – they will probably leave you weak with laughter.

Wheelbarrow race

YOU WILL NEED
- 4 or more people to race
- An open space, preferably on a soft surface

STEPS

1 FIND A PARTNER. To make a wheelbarrow, get down on all fours. Your partner then stands behind you and carefully lifts up your legs while you support yourself on your hands.

2 ON THE SIGNAL 'GO', race the other teams to the end of the course, with the wheelbarrows walking on their hands. Switch positions and race back to the starting line. The first team to get back to the starting line wins.

Three-legged race

YOU WILL NEED
- 6 or more racers
- An open area
- Bandanas, long ribbons or string

STEPS

1 SPLIT YOUR GROUP INTO PAIRS and give each pair a bandana. Standing side-by-side in pairs, tie your middle legs together, to make three 'legs' between you.

2 THEN, ON THE COMMAND 'GO', race to the end of the course and back. The team that gets back to the starting line first wins.

Egg-and-spoon race

YOU WILL NEED
- 4 or more players
- An open area
- 2 spoons
- 2 markers

- Lots of hard-boiled eggs (if you don't want to use eggs, you could use tennis balls.)

STEPS

1 FIRST, PLACE A MARKER AT THE END of the course (it's actually the half-way point because you have to go around the marker and back).

2 SPLIT INTO TWO EVEN TEAMS. On the command 'Go', the first player for each team balances an egg on her spoon and runs up to and around the marker and back to the start line, carefully balancing the egg. If she drops her egg, she must stop where she is and rebalance the egg. (If the egg is completely smashed, a team member must replace it with a new one.)

3 WHEN THE FIRST PLAYER GETS BACK to her team, she hands the egg and spoon over to the next player in line – again without dropping it. The first team to finish wins.

4 TO MAKE THINGS EVEN HARDER, you can design an obstacle course rather than a straight race. Use your imagination, but set up different stations along the route – perhaps you have to hop on one leg 10 times at one station, write your name with your 'wrong' hand at another, or sit down and stand up at another – all the while balancing that precious egg!

DID YOU KNOW? The longest egg-and-spoon race was 22 km (14 miles) and was completed in 4 hours and 17 minutes!

Playing Mahjong

✦✦✦

Mahjong is an ancient Chinese game that is now played all over the world. It is a fast and furious gambler's game and you will need lots of practice and a sharp mind if you are to master it. The name in Chinese literally means 'sparrow', because of the chirping noise made by the tiles as they're shuffled.

There are lots of variations of this popular game but, to get started, we'll discuss the basic game as played in international tournaments, which is usually played with four players. A standard set contains 144 tiles, of various different types. There are three suits: circles, bamboo and characters. Each one contains tiles from one to nine. Then there are tiles representing: three different types of dragon – red, green and white; four flowers; four seasons and four winds – north, south, east and west. There are also joker tiles, which can stand for any other type of tile, like blanks in Scrabble.

YOU WILL NEED
- Mahjong set (available in most stores that have sports and games equipment)
- 3 fellow players
- A table

STEPS

1 TO START, EACH PLAYER THROWS THE DICE and the player with the highest score goes first.

2 THE TILES ARE THEN MIXED UP and piled in 18 stacks, each one eight tiles high. The piles are laid in horizontal rows in front of each player to form a square with five piles on each side.

3 EACH PLAYER THEN TAKES 13 TILES at random from the top of the piles, and the remaining tiles are kept stacked in the middle. These are known as the wall.

4 THE OBJECTIVE IS TO COLLECT FOUR SETS of tiles in your hand, and one pair.
A set can be: three consecutive tiles in the same suit, three identical tiles, or four
of a kind. Each player takes it in turn to pick a tile from the wall, exchanging it
for a tile from her hand until she's collected all the sets.

5 THE FIRST PERSON TO GET THE COMPLETE SET is the winner, unless the wall
runs out of tiles before any players get a complete set, in which case the game
is called a draw.

If you don't feel confident enough to play with friends just yet, there are also
computer versions of Mahjong that can be downloaded and played alone. This is
a good way to get to grips with the principles of this complex game.

DID YOU KNOW? There is also a scoring system in Mahjong. Each tile
has a certain value which, when gambling, translates to a certain amount of
money that is agreed by the players. International standard rules were
formed to standardise play around the world and in 2002, the first World
Mahjong Championship was held.

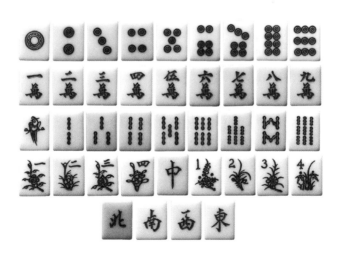

Blowing the perfect bubble

❧

Blowing the perfect bubble relies on a combination of science and magic. For the biggest, longest lasting bubbles, you need to add a magic ingredient to your detergent-and-water mix. Then, with a few clever twists of wire, you can make fantastic bubble wands and spend long, lazy days forever blowing perfect bubbles, pretty bubbles in the air . . .

YOU WILL NEED

- 2400 ml (10 cups) of water
- 960 ml (4 cups) dish-washing liquid
- 240 ml (1 cup) of glucose syrup
- A plastic-coated wire clothes hanger
- Floral netting or plastic-coated chicken wire
- Wire-cutters
- Narrow-nose pliers

STEPS

1 COMBINE THE WATER, dish-washing liquid and glucose syrup in a shallow pan, and leave the mixture to rest for a couple of hours.

2 WHILE THE MIXTURE IS RESTING, you can start making your bubble wand. Start by taking a coat hanger. Holding it by the hook, pull the opposite end down to open out the loop.

3 USING THE WIRE-CUTTERS, cut off the hook and the neck of the hanger, then straighten out the remaining wire to give you a straight length.

4 USING NARROW-NOSE PLIERS, twist a small hook at one end of the wire. Make it about as big as the wire is around – you'll see why in just a minute.

5 BEND THAT END AROUND, and hook it on to the wire about 23 cm (9 inches) from the opposite end. This should give you a circle at the end of your wand about 18 cm (7 inches) in diameter.

6 SQUEEZE THE HOOK WITH PLIERS around the wire, to keep the circle held in place, and straighten the long end of the wire. At the bottom, bunch the last few inches together to form a handle, so you get a good grip when the time comes to start making bubbles.

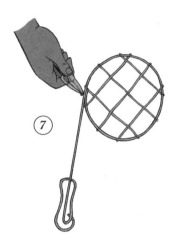

7 CUT A CIRCLE OF FLORAL NETTING OR CHICKEN WIRE about 20 cm (8 inches) in diameter. With pliers, fold the netting's edge tightly around the frame, snipping off any sharp ends. You should now have a long bubble wand with a loop at the end that has wire mesh across it.

8 HEY PRESTO! You're ready to make perfect bubbles. All you need to do to release them is dip your wand into the mixture, and either wave it through the air or blow through the mesh.

9 YOUR INSTINCT MIGHT BE to blow as hard as you can to get the biggest bubbles, but in fact blowing gently but steadily is the best way to make them grow.

DID YOU KNOW? Bubbles are spherical because of a force called surface tension, which pulls the bubble inwards around the air trapped inside.

Card tricks

Card tricks can baffle and amaze an audience. What they don't realise (nor do they ever need to know) is that tricks are really easy to do. It's more about sleight of hand than magic. With a little practice, a pack of cards and some magician's showmanship, you too can mystify the crowds.

YOU WILL NEED

- A pack of playing cards
- A volunteer

PICK A CARD . . .

1 **SHUFFLE THE CARDS THOROUGHLY,** then fan them and present them face down to your volunteer.

2 **LET HER PICK ONE** and ask her to remember what it is, but not to show you. If you like, you can ask her to show the rest of the audience. While she's doing this (and hopefully the audience is distracted), you sneak a look at the card at the bottom of the pack and remember it.

3 **INVITE YOUR VOLUNTEER** to put the card back on the top of the pack. You then cut the pack, putting the bottom half on the top. This effectively moves your volunteer's card next to the card that you've memorised from the bottom of the deck.

4 **FOR SHOW,** you can carefully cut the deck a few more times, but do not shuffle it in case you disturb your card.

5 **WHEN YOU'RE READY,** turn the pack over and scan through the deck looking for the card that you memorised. The card before it will be the one chosen by your volunteer. Draw it from the pack and show it to the audience with a flourish. Then soak up the applause.

CUTTING THE ACES

1 PLACE ALL FOUR ACES on the top of the deck before your magic show.

2 PRESENT THE DECK TO YOUR VOLUNTEER and ask her to cut it into four roughly equal piles by dropping cards from the bottom. Keep track of precisely which pile has the four aces on top.

3 POINT TO ONE OF THE NON-ACE PILES and ask your volunteer to pick it up and hold it. Ask her to take three cards from the top of the pile and place them on the bottom of the pile and then deal one card from the top of the pile on to each of the three other piles.

4 REPEAT WITH ANOTHER NON-ACE PILE and then with the final non-ace pile.

5 NOW ASK YOUR VOLUNTEER to do the same thing with the pile that has the aces in it. She'll place the top three cards onto the bottom and then deal a card onto each of the other piles.

6 WITH A FLOURISH, you then turn over the top card on each pile to reveal four aces! Now that's what I call magic!

DID YOU KNOW? Professional card-tricksters can do all sorts of clever shuffles and riffles with a pack of cards to confuse their audience and perform their tricks. Part of their skill is down to clever hands and lots of practice, but they also use a special powder called 'fanning powder' to make the cards flow smoothly over each other. The more impressed you are by a conjurer's skill with the cards, the easier it is for them to trick you!

Coin tricks

❖

If you like to mystify your friends and family, this is one of the simplest tricks in the magician's box, yet it looks very impressive when done correctly. The key to success is sleight of hand, so the advice is: practice, practice, practice.

YOU WILL NEED
- A drinking glass
- A coin
- A small hand towel
- A table
- A matchbox

DISAPPEARING COIN

1 PLACE THE COIN ON THE TABLE in full view of your audience and then turn the glass upside-down over the coin. Place the towel over the glass and, with as much drama as you can muster, move the glass around the table in circles.

2 WHILE SLIDING THE GLASS AROUND, very carefully manoeuvre it so that the coin slides off the table and into your lap (if you're sitting) or into your waiting hand. Remove the towel, and the coin has disappeared into thin air!

REAPPEARING COIN

1 BEFORE THE SHOW, open a matchbox halfway. Wedge a coin between the end of the drawer and the cover. As the applause from your disappearing coin trick dies down, produce the matchbox and, holding it tightly so the coin doesn't slip back into the box, show the audience that the box is 'empty'.

2 NOW CLOSE THE MATCHBOX, and the coin will slip down into it. Say a few magic words over the box, open it back up and – abracadabra! – your coin has magically reappeared!

Reading a palm

❖

Whether or not you believe that you can tell someone's fortune from the patterns on their palms, it's a very entertaining party trick. And who knows, perhaps you have 'the gift' and will be skilled at interpreting their personality and future.

YOU WILL NEED
- A volunteer

STEPS

1 ASK YOUR VOLUNTEER TO SHOW YOU her dominant hand (the one she writes with or uses the most). Start with her heart line. A short line suggests this is a person who is self-centred, while a long line belongs to someone who has an idealistic view of love.

2 NOW FIND THE HEAD LINE. A long straight line represents ambition with an excellent memory, whereas a short line shows a person who lacks concentration. If the line is absent, this person is very lazy, but a double line reveals a talented person with a flair for business.

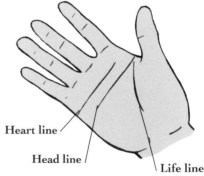

Heart line

Head line

Life line

3 FINALLY, YOU MOVE ON TO THE LIFE LINE. If it's long and deep this lucky person has lots of energy and a healthy constitution, whereas a faint line may suggest a dull and uneventful life. Any branches in the life line indicate the fortunes of that person: so if the branch goes up, there will be achievement and success, but drooping branches suggest financial and emotional misfortune – careful how you break that news to your volunteer!

Playing cat's cradle

⚜ ⚜

This is a game you can play with a chum for minutes or hours, with simple moves or very complex ones. It's great for keeping your hands occupied while you gossip.

YOU WILL NEED

- A friend

- A piece of string tied at the ends to make a circle

BASIC CRADLE

1 PUT YOUR HANDS THROUGH THE LOOP of string, making sure to keep your thumbs out of the loop. Then, by turning your hands in a circular movement, loop the string around each hand, again keeping your thumbs out of the loop.

2 PUT THE MIDDLE FINGER OF ONE HAND through the loop that is lying across the palm of the other hand and pull your hand back so that the string is taut again. Repeat with the other hand, and the resulting shape is the basic cat's cradle.

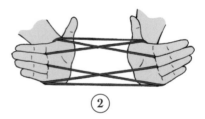

②

3 YOUR FRIEND NOW TAKES HER THUMB AND FOREFINGER and pinches the two places where the string makes an 'X' shape.

4 STILL PINCHING THE **'X'**, she lifts her hands up and apart, until the string is taut. She now points her fingers downwards and then scoops back up through the middle of the cradle, so the loops transfer to her. Then she very gently pulls. At this point, you let the string slip off your fingers and she is left with a new cat's cradle on her fingers.

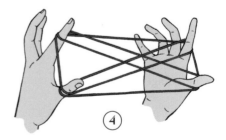

④

TRAMLINES

1 NOW, USING THUMB AND FOREFINGERS, you pinch the 'X's but approaching from the top, not the side. Still pinching the 'X's, pull your hands apart until they are outside the two outer perimeters of string.

2 STILL HOLDING THE 'X'S, push your fingers towards the middle and upwards through the middle and then pull your hands apart. The cradle should now be on your fingers, in a pattern called 'tramlines'.

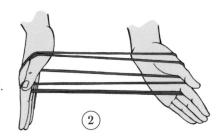

THE MANGER

1 IF YOU'RE FEELING CONFIDENT, you can try some of these more advanced shapes. After you've completed 'tramlines', it's your friend's turn again. Using her right little finger, she pulls the left single string way over to the right, beyond the outside double strings.

2 WITH THE LEFT LITTLE FINGER, she pulls the right single string to the left over the double strings, forming two little triangles.

3 WHILST HOLDING THE ENDS of the triangles tightly in her little fingers, she turns her hands and goes under the double strings with her thumb and forefinger. Without releasing the strings held by her little fingers, she spreads her thumbs and her index fingers while you let go.

DIAMONDS

1 FROM UNDERNEATH THE CRADLE, pinch the 'X's with your thumb and forefinger and pull them out. Pull them up and past the sides of the cradle and then, turning your hands over but still pinching tightly with your thumb and forefingers down, drop down through the middle.

2 STILL POINTING DOWN, spread your thumbs and forefingers apart, and *voila*, you have successfully completed cat's cradle.

German whist

There comes a time in the life of every adventurous girl when you need to fill a few hours between adventures. Whether it's mountaineers waiting for a window in the weather to conquer Everest or deep-sea divers decompressing after a voyage into the depths, most adventurers with time on their hands get out a pack of cards. So, here's how to play a favourite card game for when you've got some time to kill.

German whist

YOU WILL NEED
- A standard pack of 52 playing cards (jokers removed)
- Another player

STEPS

1 EACH PERSON IS DEALT A HAND OF 13 CARDS. The remaining cards are left in a pile on the table between you, face-down but with the top card turned over (face-up) on top of the deck. The suit of this face-up card becomes the trump suit for the game – we'll explain that in just a moment.

2 IN THE FIRST STAGE OF THIS GAME, you are trying to get good (i.e. high-value) cards from the pile to improve your hand. The non-dealer goes first. She can play any card in her hand and the other player must play a card of the same suit if possible. If she has no cards in the suit that was led, she can play any card.

3 IF BOTH CARDS ARE THE SAME SUIT, the higher card wins the trick – so a nine beats a seven, a king beats a jack, and an ace beats any other card in that suit. If the cards are of different suits, the first player wins unless the second player laid a trump card, in which case the trump wins. If two trumps are played, the higher card wins.

4 WHEN YOU WIN A TRICK, you take the face-up card on top of the pile and add it to your hand. The loser takes the next card from the pile (face-down) without showing her opponent, and adds it to her hand so that both players again have 13 cards. The two cards used in the trick are turned face down and set aside. The top card on the remaining pile is turned face up and the winner of the last trick leads the next card.

5 CONTINUE PLAYING until there are no cards left in the centre pile.

6 NOW FOR THE GAME PROPER! With the cards in your hand, you continue to play (the winner of the last trick of the first stage leads), this time without replenishing your hands. Now the aim is to win as many tricks as possible. You place your won tricks face down in front of you and whoever has the most tricks at the end of this stage wins the game.

7 DID YOU NOTICE how the tricks won in the first stage do not help you to win the second stage? Actually, all you want to do in the first stage is to collect cards in your hand that will enable you to win the most tricks in the second stage. So don't try to win an exposed card on the top of the pile if it's not very good or unless it's likely to be better than the unseen card beneath it. For example, if diamonds are trumps and the exposed card is a four of hearts, you should definitely try to lose this trick by laying one of your poorer cards. Make sense? Don't worry, it will all become clear when you start to play.

DID YOU KNOW? Variations of whist have been popular gambling games for hundreds of years. Jane Austen, Edgar Allen Poe, and Jules Verne all featured games of whist in their novels and stories.

Time capsule

❖

This is a great way to give future generations an insight into our lives, or to remind your future self of how you used to think. Fill the capsule with photographs and mementos, and put it away for as long as you like.

YOU WILL NEED
- A sturdy, weather-proof container
- Items that represent your everyday life

STEPS

1 THINK ABOUT HOW LONG you want to put your time capsule away. Is it something you want to look at in 5 years or 10, or maybe even 20? Or perhaps you'd prefer to leave it for the next generation to find?

2 DECIDE ON A SAFE PLACE TO PUT IT, bearing in mind that you may move house before the appointed time, so it shouldn't be too hard to retrieve. Your container should be waterproof, airtight and preferably fireproof. Metal tins lined with plastic bags can work well.

3 THIS COULD BE ABOUT YOU or you could get all the family involved. Get everyone to contribute photographs, letters, newspaper articles, arts and crafts, toys – in fact, just about anything that fits into the capsule.

4 WRAP EACH ITEM INDIVIDUALLY in airtight plastic bags and store the box in a cool, dry location to protect everything from decay. Leave out anything that will rot and damage other items, like rubber, wool, wood and fresh foods. If you're including electronics like CDs, remember to give instructions for how to use them, in case technology has changed by the time the box is opened.

5 INCLUDE AN INVENTORY of the items and mark everything clearly so you or someone from the future will know where each item came from and who included it when the time comes to open the capsule.

6 ONCE THE CAPSULE IS FULL and sealed, put it in its designated resting place and forget about it (well almost – at least put it out of temptation's way). Leave yourself a reminder about the time capsule in a place where you are likely to find it if you move, or if your home is damaged by a flood or fire.

7 WHY DON'T YOU ASK each family member to include a letter written to the older version of him- or herself? Mention favourite foods, music, books, movies and hobbies – you might astound yourself in years to come.

Epilogue

I can scarcely believe that we've come to the end of our adventures together. I hope that you've enjoyed them, and that you've found lots of ideas to inspire you to get out there and to have some real fun.

The great news is that you can dip into these pages as often as you like – there's always something new to try. And, as a curious girl, I'm sure you'll come up with your own great ideas for other escapades. Who knows, perhaps one day I'll be reading of your great deeds and adventures in the newspaper? And, if asked, you can say that you got your first taste for adventuring when you read this book!

Index